Victory Through the Rainbow:

Living with Pregnancy and Infant Loss

LaTanya S. Sothern

with

Michelle Cole, Aviyah A. Forrest, Kelsey Freeman, Wendy Harrell, Vianca Smith and Aisha Wilson

Sothern Education Solutions, LLC

1

ISBN 13: 978-0-692-97398-1

CONTENTS

DEDICATION

This book is dedicated to the millions of women, past and present, who have endured the loss of a child either in utero or as a neonate/newborn.

I pray that the storm you endured propels you towards your destiny, and you will intentionally find sunshine and a rainbow behind every cloud in your life.

ACKNOWLEDGMENTS

Thank you to Ms. Traxsene Martinez for her professional editing assistance.

Also, big thanks to my "creative team": my husband, T. Gregory Sothern, II, and mom Jean C. Smith, who support me in every one of my projects.

PREFACE

"What exactly is a rainbow baby?"

So many people have asked me this question as I have been on the journey to completing this book. It reminds me that unless you are a part of the "community" (so to speak) you may not know the lingo/vernacular of those of us who are. Curious eyes and concerned facial expressions usually accompany the question. The answer typically brings illumination - the eyes light up with understanding, evoking joy for some and sadness for others. A "rainbow baby" is the baby that a woman has after experiencing a pregnancy or infant loss. The concept is, having a loss during or soon after a pregnancy is like experiencing a storm in one's life and the baby is the sun that appears immediately after the storm, which then produces the rainbow - the symbol for hope, or better days ahead.

Having experienced three such losses myself, I have been blessed to have not just one but two rainbow babies. Most of my life during my 30s was spent being pregnant, recovering from pregnancy, or trying to get pregnant. Now that my child birthing years are behind me, I have been even more curious about this phenomenon around women who have a miscarriage or who lose an infant within the first year of life. How are the experiences the same? How do they differ? What do women pull on to find strength to move forward? What happens to those women who cannot?

I usually refer to this status (of having had a pregnancy or infant loss) as an involuntary sisterhood; a sorority, or secret society of sorts. It's one none of us wanted to be members of, and our "initiation" experiences were some of the most devastating moments of our lives. It is a membership we don't usually share voluntarily, until we find out about another initiate - new or otherwise. Then we open up, we swap stories, we wipe each other's tears, we grow in understanding together. There is a uniting of hearts, a feeling of, "I know what you have been through because I have been through it myself." This period can send you careening into an abyss of emotions, questions, doubts and fears. Who am I if I cannot produce a baby? Why is my body turning against me? How do I move forward with empty arms?

You as the reader may wonder, how do they escape the abyss? How does a woman pull herself up from the darkness that she finds herself in? There is no cookie-cutter solution or answer to these questions; the answers are as individual and customized as the people who have had the experiences. The women in this book have traveled to that dark abyss and have made it through. They are all at different places in their respective journeys, and there is a variety of experiences: some have gone on to have babies, some have chosen to explore adoption, and some have not had any children and are not pursuing it for whatever reason. I want the reader to understand that it is not only the losses that unite them but their resiliency through that loss, their ability to bounce back, their stories of victory in the face of certain defeat. Like that rubber band that is stretched to its maximum tensile strength, they will never be the same after their "snap back," but they know exactly how strong they are.

Here is the beautiful thing … the variety of experiences in our lives is not designed to keep us the same as before we encountered them. As living, breathing organisms we physically change and evolve daily in microscopic, almost unnoticeable ways (otherwise we cease to be). Experiences like these also force us to evolve in our mindsets and our states of emotional health. I have found that it is not our stories of defeat, but the sharing of our victories that propel us forward into greatness.

It is with this conquering spirit that I present to you seven stories of women of wonder; I like to call them "wonder wombmen." These women have overcome adversity, are now living their lives victoriously, and are the epitome of resiliency and strength. A warning to the reader - not all the stories have the socially-accepted or expected "happy ending." The stories are authentic, raw, and some are even dark. But each woman has found and held on to victory in some way.

Enjoy their journeys.

1 Rose

*A rose is the most notable and romantic of flowers. It's actually
a shrub that flowers; one whose florals are strikingly beautiful.
Although it looks fragile, it has a great defense system in the
ever-present thorn. Handle the rose carefully in order to truly
enjoy its beauty. Our Rose is beautiful but still pained, and the
thorn, as well as the pain associated with it, still remains.*

What do you dream about, hope for in your future?
What haunts you night after night when you close
your eyes and even when you're awake? I heard Oprah Winfrey say,
"Every life has a story." Kathy Lee Gifford and Hoda Kotb
incorporated it into their morning segment once a week on the Today
Show, and it resonated with me because I always believed that to truly
know someone is to know their story, their history, and their demons.
It not only gives you a window into who they are, but why they are who
they are and act the way they do. Have you ever worked with people
who you just couldn't stand, who got on your every nerve day in and

day out, who came to work and seemed to make everyone around them miserable? Then one day you find out something about their life, their family, or their past and you say, "Ooohhhh, now I get it."

Those close to me have always told me that I have a story that needs to be told. Through my anger and pain, I've wanted to tell it, but sometimes I think the main reason I wanted to tell it was to get back at those who hurt me, or so that those who were around during my "bad" days would have that "Ooohhhh" moment. However, I realized that unfortunately, it's life and some of it is a result of the decisions we make, the choices I made. Don't get me wrong. Some things knock us down that we cannot control and some that we can, but you have to get back up and keep pushing forward. Sadly, not all of us do. Some end up just existing instead of living, and some choose not to live at all.

After many years of anguish, I have had to make the conscious decision to live, even though it still is not always successfully or actively. I have had many sad days, but I live. Now I think it's time to tell my story in hopes that it will help someone else not only make the decision to live but to live enthusiastically and to not give up on life or their

dreams. Why is it that most people don't talk about it? They don't

speak of it because it is unnatural. Dr. William Petit, whose wife and

two daughters were brutally murdered in Maryland in 2007, said

something in an interview that hit me like a ton of bricks. When you

lose a spouse, society labels you as a widow or widower. When children

lose their parents, society designates them as orphans. When a parent

loses a child, what are you, who are you? There is no label and no

name. It is unnatural for parents to lose children. Unfortunately, I've

felt this too many times in my life. Whether you had your child with

you for a few days or a few months in utero, or for a few hours or years

in life, are you still a parent? And what about Mother's Day and

Father's Day? Are you still honored or acknowledged if you've lost your

child or does everyone tiptoe around you not knowing what to say or

do? If you are like me and have wanted children and expected to have

children your entire life, but can't, what then?

Genesis 1:27-28 says, *"God created man in His image, in the image of*

God He created him; male and female He created them. God blessed them; and God said to them, "Be fruitful, and multiply, and fill the earth, and subdue it…" This command from God Himself told me that it was not only natural but also expected for women to have children, that we are here to be fruitful, multiply and replenish the earth. And for as long as I can remember, I wanted to have children - as many as possible. I wanted to "be fruitful, and multiply, and fill the earth." My paternal grandmother had ten children, and when I was about seven or eight years old, I thought that was a good number to strive for; I wanted to have about ten children like my grandmother. However, as I grew older, and came to my senses, I thought five or six would be the number of children my husband and I would have. Some are thinking – that's coming to your senses! Hahahaha! I had even decided that after my husband and I had all of the biological children we wanted, we would adopt a child to give someone else's child a good home. Yes, I knew all of this by the time I was a young teenager. Now as an adult, if I couldn't do this, why was I here? Who was I? What did my future hold?

I looked up to my paternal grandmother and always wanted to be like her. She and my grandfather did not have much money, but they had a lot of love to give to their lot of children. My grandmother was an incredible woman. She didn't talk much, was very soft spoken and docile, but she had a phenomenal presence. Although she was quiet, she exuded an incredible love and strength. And when I was older, I realized just how strong she truly was. She and my grandfather were married sixty-two years, and of those ten children they had together, they lost three. In those days, when a child was born the doctor would put a clamp on the umbilical cord after it was cut. The clamp caused an infection in one of their sons, and he died 72 hours later. I can physically imagine my grandmother's pain. They also had two daughters who both died from Diphtheria; one was eight months old, and the other was three years old. But, growing up no one talked about those additional three children.

I didn't know about my father's three siblings until after my second pregnancy, and I wished my grandmother was around for me to talk to about them and what she went through, how she felt and how she went on. When I found this out, I just wanted to hug my grandmother; I wanted to be in her presence. Then I just thought about her smile; she always had this faint soft smile. Now I wonder if her smile was genuine or if she was masking the hurt inside. I guess the other seven children still made her smile though. I suppose; maybe; one would hope.

At 19, I married my childhood sweetheart, my best friend whom I had known since I was 12. We could talk for hours, always had fun and just knew we would be together forever. We got engaged just before he left to go to basic training for the United States Army when I was 18, then a year later we had a fairytale wedding. We had nine bridesmaids, nine groomsmen, two flower girls and a ring bearer, and we rode in a 1935 Rolls Royce. Everything was perfect until we decided to "be fruitful, and multiply, and fill the earth."

In just under a year after we married, in what seemed like the natural progression of our lives together, we were pregnant. This pregnancy was the best news, and everyone we knew was so excited. It was to be the first grandchild for my parents. My husband was the youngest of seven, and his family was ecstatic in anticipation of their tenth grandchild, but their baby boy's first child. We were all so excited and couldn't wait to add to our family. I knew from the very beginning that it was a boy; I always knew from the first movement, the first kick what the sex of my child would be. It was later confirmed by ultrasound, and my husband was over the moon, constantly bragging to everyone he came in contact with that he was going to have a son. Little did we know that this was the end of our fairytale and the beginning of our horror story.

I had always been very healthy, and the doctors did not expect any problems. I had morning sickness, which I believe, should be renamed. After all of these years of women suffering and for most, IT IS ALL DAY. (In fact, that may be my next project - I'll start a petition to have "morning sickness" renamed.) Wow, I can remember that part like it was yesterday. I would go to lunch with my co-workers and within thirty minutes, just go and stand in the bathroom because I knew what was about to happen. But actually, even the "morning sickness" was a joy to me because I knew I was creating life; that my child was growing inside of me. I started out at 5'0" and about 105 lbs,

7

and everyone I crossed paths with told me how much I glowed. I was so proud to be pregnant.

But very quickly, I began to round out, and after three months, I had gained about 10 pounds. When I went to the doctor for my regular prenatal visit, the doctors told me that it was normal for first-time mothers to gain a lot of weight; that I should just cut back on my eating. Although I tried to explain that I was not eating much and what I was eating did not stay down, the weight gain was dismissed by my doctor. I faithfully kept my scheduled appointments, and I continued to gain more and more weight and showed signs of swelling in my hands and feet, but nothing seemed alarming to the doctor. At about 22-23 weeks, I felt awful. I was huge, had gained about 30 lbs., and was sick all day. It was a Friday, and I called my doctor. The doctor told me I probably had a stomach virus and that I should try to eat dry toast and drink tea. I was furious because I felt they were just dismissing me and my complaints. I had decided that I was going to the office first thing Monday morning and force someone to examine me because I knew it was more than just a stomach virus. Even if she thought it was a stomach virus, I now know the doctor should have told me to come in for an exam since I was just shy of six months in my pregnancy and had gained almost 40 lbs.

Then all hell broke loose, and I didn't make it to Monday. One fall Sunday my husband and I were enjoying a football game and dinner at his sister's house; I began to get extremely sick. I had quickly developing pain in my lower back and could not stop vomiting. At first, everyone joked that it was my sister-in-law's cooking, but it didn't stop. My husband decided to take me to the emergency room, an HMO, which was the first hospital of the night. I walked into the ER on my own, and as the attendant was taking my vitals, she seemed to be frustrated with my not being able to pinpoint the pain and give her more details as to why I was there. She kept asking a lot of questions, and I was just scared and in pain. She wanted to know exactly where the pain was and how severe it was. She wanted to know exactly when the pain started and how long it had been happening. The attending physicians finally told my husband that they did not see anything seriously wrong, but that he should take me to the women's hospital about ten minutes away since I was pregnant. (Ya think?)

My husband put me back in our car and drove me to the women's hospital, now hospital number two of the night. My condition had begun to deteriorate, and I could no longer walk on my own. My husband had to get a wheelchair to get me inside the hospital. The pain was severe, I could not stop vomiting, and the swelling was getting worse. After being examined and asked pretty much the same questions as the attendant from the first hospital, they knew what was wrong with me almost immediately, but said that it was so advanced, there was no one there experienced enough to handle my case. Now, I was being sedated and "stabilized" to prevent seizures so that I would survive the ambulance ride to the third hospital of the night, about 15-20 minutes away, where there was a specialist who had experience with Eclampsia.

Yes, they finally gave it a name; not a stomach virus. I had Eclampsia and was in pre-term labor at 24 weeks. By the time I reached the specialist, he said that I had the worst case of Eclampsia he had seen in ten years. He was shocked that my obstetrician had not picked up on the signs and done something sooner (the weight gain and the swelling that I had complained about). And were they even taking note of my blood pressures during my appointments? They did urine tests each time; did they check my kidney function? Both probably showed signs all along because now both numbers were through the roof.

At 21, after being married for just over a year, my husband was told to decide if he wanted to try to save his wife first or our son; he had to choose while looking at his wife whom he could barely recognize and who was slowly dying in front of him. He had to have been terrified, especially with my mother standing there beside him ready to put him in a hospital bed if he made the wrong decision. The doctors could leave my son inside me, in utero, to give his lungs a week or two more to develop; to give him a better chance of survival and lower the likelihood of physical and mental disabilities, BUT I would most likely die as my organs continued to shut down. They would have to keep my body functioning on life support to sustain him. Or, they could do a C-section to deliver my son, which would lessen the stress on my body and my organs to save my life. They would then put him in an incubator to hopefully continue his development. However, delivering my son at 24 weeks not only lessened his chance of survival but only increased my chances by a small percentage. What a "choice"! At 21 years old, what was he to do?

I can say now; thankfully my husband chose the C-section to try to save my life, although I have had days, many days where I wished he hadn't. But wait! I had to overcome yet another hurdle. As they started the surgery to deliver my son, my lungs began to collapse, and they had to stop. It took them hours to stabilize me to deliver my baby. My nightmare started on Sunday evening, and my tiny, feisty son was born at 3:51 p.m. on Monday, November 3, 1986, and weighed in at 1lb. 4 oz. He was incredible, but just as the doctors thought, his little lungs were not as developed as they needed to be. He was in an open incubator and on a ventilator. Ventilators back then were not made for such small babies; they were huge, and the pumping was too forceful for such small bodies. Every day, the doctors and nurses expected it to be his last. He, on the other hand, had other ideas. He fought each and every day. Although he never got worse, he never got any better.

I was semi-conscious for about two and a half days and did not see my son until he was three days old. When they first told me he was born at 3:51, I, of course, thought it was a.m. because I didn't realize how much time had gone by since I was admitted. I had no idea of all that had occurred that took his delivery into the next day. I remember very little about his birth. I remember briefly waking up in the ambulance having no idea what was going on; then I remember brief moments of consciousness with our family sitting around me in the hospital room. I remember my oldest sister-in-law feeding me ice chips and family members praying. Finally, tired, weak and in pain from the emergency C-section and all of the poking and prodding, I was able and ELATED to see my son. I believe he held on for me. At this point, he probably thought he only had a father and all these other people. Now, he got to meet his mother, hear the muffled voice that he heard for six months.

My brother-in-law, who was a Pastor, visited my son every day of his short life. You would have thought he was his son. One day as I lie in my hospital room, I caught a glimpse of what looked like my brother-in-law rushing past my hospital room door. I yelled out to him, and he came back and spoke, but as he poked his head in he said he would see me later; he had to see my son first. I just laughed and was so grateful for all of the people who were praying for all three of us. My husband grew up in the church, and he and his family introduced me to true Christianity, not just religion, but the love of God. But here I was, a baby in Christ facing an unbearable test of faith. I needed all of our family members.

Every day, I wheeled to the Neonatal Intensive Care Unit (NICU), and I would sit beside my son's incubator and talk to him, and stroke his tiny hands, fingers, and head. He always knew it was me. Whenever the nurses needed to change his tubes or bandages, he would squirm and kick his little legs. But if I were there touching him or talking to him while they did it, he would be just as still as he could. Babies know their mothers. They learn your voice, breathing, and heartbeat, and he could feel that it was me. He was a mama's boy, though he looked like the both of us. I jokingly called him ET because he was so tiny with those long fingers. One day, I got the best gift; they let me hold him. Tubes were everywhere, but I got to do what all mothers long for, hold him in my arms. Sitting in the NICU beside his incubator, I would always ask him to open his eyes; I needed to see his eyes.

But there was this one nurse who tried to destroy my hopes. She told me that he would never open his eyes because he was too premature and she was surprised he had made it that long. Every time she was in the NICU, as this nurse left she would say she didn't expect to see him when she came back on duty. I wanted to run her down with my wheelchair and back over her.

After about a week and a half, the doctors were ready to release me from the hospital. I did not want to leave because I didn't want to be away from my son, and I almost didn't - ANOTHER

UNEXPECTED HURDLE. The day I was to be discharged, I was dressed and waiting for the doctor on call to check me out.

The doctor came into my room and told me that he needed to look at my incision from the C-section before I left, and give my husband and me instructions on the care of it. He began poking and pushing on my incision, and the next thing I knew I was screaming. If I could have moved, I would have gotten off that hospital bed and beaten the crap out of that doctor! As he was checking my incision, he saw a bit of blood oozing and used a long Q-tip to OPEN the incision. A Q-tip! The nurse heard the commotion and came running into the room. Apparently, the oozing blood signaled more old blood, a blood clot just underneath the first layer of the incision and he needed to reopen it and clean it out to avoid infection. I would hope a more professional, more experienced doctor would have explained what he needed to do before doing it with no pain medication, and waited for the nurse. An explanation would have only taken a few minutes, and infection would not have set in within the time it took him to explain what he needed to do. The nurse had to give me a shot for the pain

16

quickly. Needless to say, I didn't go home that day. Talk about growing up!

Good news though! That mean, horrible nurse was wrong. After about two weeks, my son opened his eyes just for me, and he fought and lived for 25 days. In the end, the respirator was just too much for his tiny heart to endure. My husband and I received a dreadful telephone call from the hospital about 2:00 a.m. that our son had lost his fight at 1:30 AM on November 28, 1986. He was the first of our FIVE children who are all now in heaven: one miscarriage at eight weeks, two beautiful stillborn daughters at 23 and 24 weeks, and our beautiful daughter born almost in the same way as her older brother at 27 weeks on November 2, 1989. Her birthday was the day before her brother's, and she lived for five days.

Who am I if I can't "be fruitful, and multiply, and fill the earth?" That question plagues me every day of my life. Over the years, I have counseled and helped other women dealing with fertility issues, and it made me feel good knowing that I was able to give them the information they couldn't seem to get from anyone else. Maybe no one else made them feel comfortable enough to talk about it. Many went on to have children off of my advice.

So where does that leave me? For many years, I put all of my focus on my nieces and nephew. I doted on them and was so proud to watch them grow into incredible adults. They were my saving grace; they saved my life and my sanity. After they grew older, I would not, could not go near a child under the age of about five. I would not go to hospitals or baby showers. I would send gifts to my friends, but never saw the joys of their lives. I tried to live in a world where children just were not prevalent, which mainly existed from my home to my job. I migrated more to friends who did not have children, and I just tried not to focus on my loss, the longing and aching for children.

At 50 years old, I had a hysterectomy, and that was probably the first time I realized I would truly not have a child. Until then, I think my mind held on to the possibility, even if it was with technology and not entirely and biologically mine, that someday my dream would come true. I think I watched too many Lifetime movies where there is always a happy ending. And with so many celebrity women coming out about pregnancies and births much later in life, it gives other women the illusion that it can be the norm for them too – until it's not.

I have learned to rejoice in small victories in my life, such as my job, a few close friends and still being alive with a smidge of sanity, but not much else. I am grateful to my niece because she shares her family with me and makes me feel a part of it as much as possible. When I couldn't be close to or hold any other child, I couldn't NOT hold hers. Every day, my prayer is for God to guide me to my purpose, to show me where He would have me to be and what He would have me to do. If I'm completely real with myself, I can see some of what He's had me to do. I haven't been on one job where there wasn't someone who has benefited from my story, my trials, and my advice. Maybe it's time for me to see a different purpose. Maybe I am instrumental in "being fruitful, multiplying, and filling the earth," but just in a different way than I saw growing up.

2 AMBER

*Amber is a fossilized tree resin that hardens over time.
Primarily, it is a preservative, and protects the contents it
encases. It has been noted for its beauty and transformed into
jewelry, but has also been used for its healing properties. Our
Amber had to be a preserver in the midst of her pain, and so
begins her story.*

"**B**abe I'm bleeding!"

He responded, "What do you mean you're bleeding?"

"I'm bleeding, and it's bad. I Googled, and I read that slight

bleeding and spotting is normal for the first couple of weeks. I don't

think this is normal bleeding!" I was starting to become concerned.

Like all little girls, I had dreams of what my life would be when

I grew up. I imagined that everything would be perfect. My husband

would be incredibly handsome and wealthy; we would live in a ten-bedroom mansion in the suburbs or Rock Creek Park (I'm from DC),

I'd drive a Mercedes Benz, have one perfect child and live happily ever

after. And just like all little girls you never really think about what all

that means. How will of this happen? Where do you meet prince

charming and does he exist? As you grow older, so do your thoughts

and reasoning. You begin to realize that life is not always what you

dreamed it would be and that there are certainly obstacles along the way

of getting your happily ever after.

Dreams are supposed to come true, right? I never imagined

that my dream would become a real live nightmare. After all, I love and

worship God; I'm faithful if I just believe and pray everything will work

out. Well, things did eventually work out just not the way I planned

(with the emphasis on "I"). We get so caught up our plans and how

things are "supposed" to happen - in a specific way at a specific time -

that we often miss the blessings and miracles that are happening around

us. My husband and I almost did, but I thank God for the people

around us who can help you see through the fog of your

disappointments, fears, confusions, and anger to help you put everything into perspective.

First Comes Love

For as long as I can remember I have always wanted to attend Eastern Senior High in Washington, DC. Growing up, I didn't know anybody first hand who attended, but there was always something that attracted me to the grandeur of the building and the students I would see walking in and out of the building as my grandma and I drove by every day. I would declare every day that one day I'm going to go there and I'm going to be a cheerleader. Everyone will know me, I'll have a "fine" boyfriend, and we'll be high school sweethearts, get married and have babies. Somehow, even as a child, I could feel the importance of speaking what I wanted or saying my dreams out loud.

Well, in 1996 (school year '96/'97) I entered Eastern High School as a bright-eyed freshman with high hopes of accomplishing everything I said I would at the school. I got to know everyone in my homeroom and classes, I hung out with upperclassmen from my old middle school to get to know other people, and before you know it, it was cheerleading tryout time. I had all the confidence in the world because my cheerleading coach from elementary school and middle school was the new cheerleading coach at Eastern. I thought, "Oh I got this, it will be 'sweat less,'" and then, heartbreak.

My mom wanted me to focus more on school and to get good grades, so she did not allow me to try out for the team. I was CRUSHED. I was more than crushed I was distraught and heartbroken. I had to sit back and listen to my friends talk about tryouts and hear their names being called over the intercom knowing that I was supposed to be one of them. It hurt down to my very core. I thought nothing could ever hurt this bad. Little did I know more was coming in my future, but we'll get to that later.

That year went on, I got good grades just like my mom asked me too. I made great friends along the way. I was able to try out for cheerleading the next year, and of course, I made the squad. On the day of my very first game, I noticed my friend walking with a boy I had never seen. Later I asked all the questions a girl who is clearly interested would ask. What's his name? What grade is he in? What' neighborhood is he from? Are you all together? She answered all of the questions with everything I wanted to hear, and from that point on, everything was just a matter of chance and possibilities. As chance would have it one of the very good friends I had made turned out to be one of his best friends. I will never forget sitting in Health, and Human Resources class bored out of my mind talking about this guy who I thought was fine, mentioning his name and my friend saying, "JAMAL? That's my dog! I got you; this is going to be easy."

And that it was. In a matter of weeks, we had met, exchanged numbers and began the high school dating process. It was magical. We dated for the remainder of my years spent at Eastern. He was there when I turned 16; we went to each other's proms, he was truly my first real boyfriend, first love, first everything.

We had dreams of getting married and starting a family after college. The only problem was he was a year ahead of me, and I did not like ANY of his college choices. He didn't leave for college right away, which made things easier for us. Eventually, he went away to school, and we entered a new stage: the long-distance relationship, which worked fine for a while. The challenge came when I left for school, and I was serious about making good grades as I had always been. It became harder to focus on a long-distance relationship and school, and so we parted ways. We both entered different relationships later on, some successful some not, but there was always a special place in my heart for my first love.

To sum up our dating journey, we reconnected before I graduated from college, began dating again and everything was going just as we had imagined. I graduated from college, got my dream job but felt like something was missing in my life. I was looking for a deeper spiritual connection than what I currently had. I had attended church all my life but didn't feel like I was "being fed" the way I needed to. Jamal was feeling the same way and told me about a church his sister had been attending and mentioned the idea of us going to visit. Needless to say, I was there that very next Sunday with my best friend in tow; my best friend who just happened to be the same girl I had questioned about Jamal in high school. I loved every single thing about the ministry. It was fresh and exciting. There was worship, the people were friendly, the preacher was a bit more radical than what I was used to (which I must admit in the beginning threw me off a bit), but at the same time, it was very attractive. I found myself sitting in the pews every week and loving the Word I was hearing that was steeped in faith and trust in God, studying the Word to get to know God for myself, and developing a relationship with Him that would catapult my life into new dimensions that I had never imagined. Of course, that spoke to me because I was a dreamer and wanted all my dreams to come true.

I joined the church after about a month of visiting, and Jamal joined not much long after. We dated for about three years while applying the Word to our lives and allowing it to transform our thinking and manner of doing things completely. We stopped having sex and even stopped kissing so it would not lead to sex. It was intense, but we were serious about our walk. We knew we wanted to get married and our thought was if we could honor God with our bodies, and or lifestyles, then He would honor us in our marriage, and the entire marriage would be blessed. We'd have no worries, and everything would be perfect. We entered marital counseling and were officially engaged about a month before counseling ended.

Then Comes Marriage

On April 7, 2007, we were married in our church by our pastor in front of all of our loved ones. It was a day filled with love, joy, peace and it was everything I hoped it would be. We started our journey to a family on this day. We immediately began to plan how we wanted to the process to work: when we would start trying, how many kids we wanted, names, godparents everything. By the end of all the planning, the decision was made to wait until we had been married for five years and then we would begin to try. This was the first process that didn't go as planned.

Around year two I started to get the itch. I was teaching kindergarten, and volunteering in the nursery at church, which sent me into baby heaven. However, hubby was NOT having it. So the waiting process began. There were a few "scares" in between, but we made no purposeful efforts until the end of 2011 and all through 2012. Trying to have a baby can put significant stress on a relationship if you let it. Some people have even said that sex changed for them because it became more about the end goal versus continuing to enjoy the experience of the act with their partner. The same was true for us.

Though our relationship remained intact, there was stress individually especially for me. We had been trying for only about two months, and I could not understand why it wasn't happening. I was praying; I stopped taking the pill, bought information books, I had to convince Jamal to have sex in a particular position, the whole nine yards. GOD, why is this not working?

I remember calling my sister every time I had a symptom. "Tan, I feel woozy is that a symptom?" "Tan, sleep has just been falling on me like crazy. Isn't that a symptom? "OMG LaTanya, I can't stop eating I KNOW that's a symptom." She would often laugh or reassure me that yes it was a symptom but symptoms do not mean you're pregnant. I would roll my eyes, (without her knowing of course), call her a killjoy and call a friend. I was just desperate for anyone to tell me, "Yes girl you are pregnant." Instead, my friend insisted, "You know, the mind is a powerful tool." I was completely shocked. Your friend is supposed to tell you what you want to hear. Not let you down easy. On to the next friend.

By the time I had reached my fourth friend within two days of calling, and three to four months of starting the process of trying, I was completely distraught that I did not see a positive sign on those pregnancy tests. It was heartbreaking. So, to put things into perspective and get solid advice, I called a friend who had also had challenges getting pregnant. She too said some of the same things that my sister and other friends had mentioned, but she added advice. She recommended that I purchase the book, "Supernatural Childbirth" in expectation of no pain or other discomforts that people go through during childbirth. I told her, "You know I'm willing to do what you say, but I have to ask - why should I get a book on childbirth when I'm trying to get pregnant. Shouldn't I get a book on that?" She went on to say that this book will help me believe beyond just the pregnancy and towards delivering a child. The book would help me expand my belief. See, our pastor taught us that what you focus on will expand, so only believing for the pregnancy is half the battle.

If I could begin to believe toward the end goal of delivery, getting pregnant would be easy. My friend also encouraged me to relax and let it happen naturally. Many times, putting too much energy and thought into one thing will breed anxiety and as many of us know anxiety and stress do not mix in pregnancy or even when trying to get pregnant. I took her advice, I bought the book began to read, didn't think about getting pregnant and within a month I saw a positive pregnancy test.

Then comes me with the baby carriage

It was the moment we had believed for. I couldn't wait to tell my husband. In my mind, I would plan this "Full House" creative way to tell him he was going to be a dad, but I was so overwhelmed with joy and love and excitement I couldn't wait for that I had to tell him right then and there. I rushed into the room woke him out of his sleep and blurted it out. He smiled a half sleep smile, hugged me and said, "yaaaaaay!" I gave him a pass because he was completely knocked out. I didn't even care I was excited for the both of us. I began to text my sister and of course the friend whose advice I had heeded and my two BFF's. They all gave me the response I was looking for. It was incredible, I was going to be a mommy, and it felt incredible.

It's amazing how soon you began to feel like a mother and connect with your baby. From the moment I saw the positive sign, everything changed. I had to catch myself because I even began to walk cautiously. You immediately become over protective and careful of what you do. Some of my friends say I am the google queen, it has to be true because I began to google EVERYTHING. How much sleep a pregnant person needed, all the foods I was eating, especially coffee, how soon to go to the doctor EVERYTHING. I also signed up for a pregnancy website that keeps track of how far along you are, what to expect each week and what the baby looks like as it develops each week. Between Google, the website, and my sister (who is my own personal "Google") I was set. Well, at least I thought I was.

Sometimes too much information isn't useful. I had so much

information that I became paranoid and worried, which causes stress,

and, like I said before, stress and pregnancy don't mix at all. I had to

purposefully keep myself calm and only look up information that was

necessary for the moment.

Well, that moment came rather quickly. Around one to two

weeks after I found out I was pregnant I began to feel cramps, which

my research told me was normal. Of course, after Google, I asked my

sister and friends with young kids, and they all said cramping CAN be

normal. A few would ask do the cramps feel like period cramps or

worse than your typical period cramps? I was so nervous about what

my answer should be that I really couldn't give an honest response. I

wanted to respond with whatever would have them respond with, "yes

that's normal." However, I gave as honest of an answer that I could.

"They're about the same." They all said pretty much the same thing, "I

can't tell you your cramps are normal. I can just believe God with you

that everything is fine." So NOT what I wanted to hear. A couple of days later bleeding accompanied the cramps. Not a lot of blood but enough for me to worry.

I told my husband what was going on and that I thought I should go to the emergency room because it had been happening for a couple of days and the blood is bright red not pink. We hopped in the car, prayed for the best possible outcome and made our way to the hospital. Sitting in the waiting room was pure torture. I tried my best to hold on to what I was believing, and I wish I could say I was as cool as a cucumber, but I wasn't. Well on the outside you couldn't tell anything was wrong, but on the inside, I was screaming and crying.

The nurse called my name, and the process began. They took blood work, and I had to get a vaginal sonogram since I was only a couple of weeks pregnant. The sonogram was so uncomfortable and nerve wracking. While they were looking everything over, the technician kept clicking and squinting and counting. I heard the Holy Spirit say, "They found two babies." She called her supervisor in, and they counted again. The supervisor confirmed, "Yes I see it too." I asked is everything ok? She told me that she couldn't give me any information in the room but assured me as soon as I got to my room the doctor would tell me everything.

We got down to the room, I told my husband what I had heard from Holy Spirit, and sure enough, when the doctor came, she confirmed. She held up a picture of my uterus and said, "You see that little circle there?" I responded, "yes," she said, "Well that's your baby, and you see this circle over here?" I slowly replied, "Yes." She replied, "Well that's your other baby!" My husband and I could not believe what we were hearing. How In the world did this happen? The doctor went on to explain more to us. She told us that unfortunately they also found that I had uterine fibroids, four to be exact. They were all the size of oranges and would either get bigger, stay the same size or burst. Either way, there was not enough room in there for the fibroids and two growing babies, so the blood I was experiencing was more than likely from one or both of the babies beginning the process of miscarrying. Just like that our unexpected happy moment was now the exact opposite. We were crushed. How could this happen to us? We did everything we were supposed to do: I was eating right, I was believing for a supernatural pregnancy. It just didn't make sense. We decided right then to jump into action.

I texted the First Lady of my church to tell her what was happening, and she immediately ministered to me and began believing with me. I gathered scriptures from the book and wrote them on my mirror and began to confess them daily. I was on a mission. I was determined that the devil would not win this fight and I would have two babies. Days and weeks went on, but the blood didn't stop, neither did the cramping. I visited the ER more times than I could count. I never gave up hope, never stopped confessing, didn't mention to anybody who wouldn't be in faith with us and continued to believe God that what had been started in me would finish. I never doubted that my pregnancy would end prematurely but that I would go all the way.

I eventually had to tell the supervisors at my job what was happening because I was visiting the ER so much I began to miss a considerable amount of days from work. I was on medication for pain, and blood clots were starting to occur. It was not easy to believe through what I was seeing, and I was looking for someone to tell me that everything was normal, to tell me that this happens, but it's ok. I was never able to get that response from anyone. I remember visiting my sister because she was spoiling me oh so terribly. When the first huge blood clot came, I called the doctor, and he instructed me to take pics and gather it. I couldn't believe I had to collect evidence. I would pray and do what I was instructed to do. I went in for yet another visit, and the babies were still there. One day I was at work in excruciating pain. I still to this day don't know how I taught a room full of first graders, 13 of which were six-year-old boys, by myself from 7:45 am until 3:30 pm, in as much pain as I as in that day. I went to the bathroom after dismissal, and the worst thing that I could have ever imagined happened right before my eyes. A clot that was the biggest so far in the shape of a tiny child was in the toilet. I immediately knew what had just taken place. I used all the strength that I could muster up to flush the toilet and tell my boss I had to go to the ER. She looked at me as if she knew; I began to cry uncontrollably and headed to the ER.

When I arrived, I had just finished a conversation with a friend who MADE me gather myself and finish the fight. "Continue strong, believe in spite of what it looks like." So, I was pumped and ready to face the doctors. They confirmed that I had lost one and searched for what seemed like an hour for the other. When they were just about to give up, one of the objects they thought was a fibroid began to move. They were able to catch the heart rate frequency on the monitor and confirm that the second baby was still there and very much alive. So much so it was jumping. The baby didn't have developed fingers and feet yet, but it was jumping. I found myself very conflicted. Feeling heartbroken that one child was gone but incredibly grateful to have another. I was faced with a decision. I could either wallow in sadness for the one I lost or rejoice and continue to fight for the one that remained. I don't even have to tell you what choice I made. I started the biggest faith fight of my life to date right then and there.

My doctor requested to see me weekly since I was I considered high risk now, just to check the baby's heart beat and make sure everything was ok. Of course, every week it was. I continued to say my confessions, my husband and I picked out names. I continued to buy baby clothes and diapers because I knew I was going to bring a baby home who would fill it. Every week I went to that doctor's office confident that we would hear a heartbeat and every week I did. I was in a continual state of thanksgiving and unrelenting faith. We never even told our parents about the process that was happening. We couldn't afford for the emotions and worry to hinder our faith.

Through all of the "scares" we endured (like how on Christmas I fell and spent the entire day in the hospital monitoring the baby), and the brief moments of worry, we continued to trust God that we would have a supernatural delivery and bring our healthy baby home. There was absolutely no other option for us. On April 6th around 7 am I started having contractions. We went to the hospital but were sent home. Around 4 pm the contractions had gotten worse and were close, and I knew it was different from the morning. We went to the hospital; they confirmed it was labor and the process had begun. After about 14 hours of labor and an emergency C-section. Zoe Lanay Smith arrived at 7:11 am on April 7, 2013, weighing in at 7lbs 5oz. One day after my 5th wedding anniversary (remember we said we would wait five years).

The entire experience taught me how to believe God and never stop fighting. I can look at my story in many different ways, but I choose to be thankful. I have a testimony that many women have: in spite of a miscarriage I was still able bring home a healthy baby from the same pregnancy. That statement isn't to put anyone else down or even make anyone feel bad, it only shows and reminds me how to focus on the positive. I have found myself faced with challenges after this where I have had no choice but to believe God through it. On some occasions, I would "trip." Then, I'd hear my daughter's voice and remember that I've been through worse and made it to the other side.

Zoe (her name means "life") is four years old now and is the absolute joy of our lives. She's charismatic, brilliant, super loving and an awesome big sister. That's right I've even had the opportunity to carry another child with no problems during the pregnancy or delivery because I knew how to believe God for the best favorable outcome and not doubt that it would come to pass. Jamal David Smith was born on April 20, 2015. Yes, both of our babies were born in April.

What can I say, I'm a teacher I have the summers off. Hehe.

3 SUNNI

Yellow is the color of hope. People use yellow ribbons to indicate they are hopeful that a loved one will return. Children use the color yellow to create big, hopeful suns in their pictures. It's this hope that we draw from to push us through difficult situations. It's this same hope that our Sunni depends on to push her forward in her quest to not just have a baby, but to become a mother.

I can't just "move on" (in fact, those words make me angry), I never will. I will never forget the extreme joy I felt when I tested that first time and got a positive pregnancy test. I was crying, and dancing, and running around the house freaking out that "I'm going to be a MOM!" I will never forget the pregnancy symptoms that I had, and how I got sick after everything I ate and then how brushing my teeth after would just make me sick all over again. I will never forget how I hated sweets and couldn't stand the sight or smell of them. I will not forget when I purchased jeans with an elastic waist and was overjoyed at the fact that I got to wear them. I will never forget watching my belly grow and how my usual absent mind, never missed a weekly bump picture. I will not forget spending hours making secret boards on Pinterest and searching for everything baby, for that specific little one. I will never forget the days we realized our babies had slipped away so suddenly. I will never forget how still receiving those emails with "Congrats, your baby is the size of…" or the latest sale at Pea in a Pod could make me so angry.

I swear I've tried to unsubscribe from all things mommy, but somehow, they still kept sneaking through the cracks. Didn't they know I didn't need these things anymore or the reminder that I didn't? I'll never forget the feeling of limbo you're left in like it never even happened (after all you have nothing to show for it other than your broken heart) mixed with feeling like it's still happening to you and won't stop. Never.

I can remember every last detail, of each one of my pregnancies. Every single one. And the moments that lead up to the moment we learn all my hopes for our little family I had dreamed up and that had become a reality to me when I saw that positive test were shattered. I can remember the ultrasound technician's glazed-over look as she rolled the wand over my belly. I remember the sweeping look of fear that covered my husband's face. I remember the pain of a full bladder that was usually tolerable because I was too busy watching the screen, but they turned the screen out of my sight. How badly I just wanted them just to tell me what I already knew from all the non-verbal cues. I remember waiting for what felt like days but was, in reality, probably only a few minutes. I remember wringing my hands over and over –just numb ... already knowing what was to come; waiting to be told me that I wouldn't be "going home" with my baby.

I still remember the walk of shame out the door of the doctor's office. The nurse that had been full of smiles on the way back to the exam room, now looked at the floor as she held the door open for me to leave. The super sweet receptionist that had chatted with me about how I was feeling, now did not speak to me as she handed me copies of my medical records to take to the OR. No one would look at me in the eyes because, of course, they all knew that I was one of those unfortunate souls who just got "The Bad News." Each time we received the news that I had prayed so hard I wouldn't hear, I would hold it together out of this sense that I couldn't make others feel more uncomfortable that I already had. I would keep it together until that car door would shut, and then I sobbed. Screamed. I wanted my baby back and to be thriving inside me. I wanted my body to be a healthy home. But I couldn't make it happen.

My heart would sink within me. I would feel a weakness come over me. I had no control over what had happened; I'd done nothing 'wrong.' But why? Why again? And now I was left to deal with all these emotions and a sweet husband with another mascara-drenched shirt. And despite his own broken heart, he couldn't understand the pain my body was experiencing. My pregnancy, the one that's supposed to be filled with anticipation and excitement ended in heartbreak and mortality.

It's impossible to forget. Each one of our little ones was a part of me, a part of us, and although they weren't able to make their grand entrance into the world to stay, they have surely made their grand

entrance in my heart forever.

The word "miscarry" makes me cringe, and not for the typical

stereotypes associated with it. The prefix "mis" holds a negative

connotation that implies bad or wrongly. Even though I understand the

underlying meaning of the word, I did not wrongly or badly carry my

babies - in fact, I would have done anything to hold onto that life.

My heart just breaks, because this word becomes misleading for

women who find themselves in the midst of what is already such a

devastating event. It is so easy and even natural to make the jump to "I

was bad," "I did wrong," and "This is why my baby died." We find

ourselves securitizing every detail of the pregnancy trying to find that

moment of fault and where we went wrong. Was it that one extra cup

of coffee? Did I roll on my belly while I was sleeping? Was I too

stressed? Any ridiculous explanation I could fathom to explain how it

was indeed my fault. In the thick of it, it is so hard to wrap your mind around the fact that a term like "miscarriage" doesn't define the person going through it.

As I've continued to process the past and look forward to the future, I've realized that there are so many aspects of loss that I never understood until it happened to me. The loss has come in many forms for me over the last four years, from early miscarriages to babies well into their second trimesters, to birth moms that have changed their mind about their ability to place their child for adoption. Whether I knew about these little ones for a few days, months or wasn't the one carrying him/her in my belly, I was never prepared for the heartbreak and what would follow. And in all honesty, it would catch me off guard each time, with how much it would just utterly crush me no matter how much I prepared myself. I am not saying anyone's experience was less important, or I loved that little one less but I knew what was coming and what to expect and, well, part of me had protected myself during the "wait." I feel guilty, but also heartbroken for the excitement that has been replaced with fear because of our losses. When I think back to the joy those first ultrasound appointments brought, versus the sense of pain and dread experienced in my subsequent pregnancies; that just waiting for the other shoe to drop feeling. Don't get me wrong, I am usually a very glass half full kind of girl, but that first loss took a piece of my heart and with each that followed more was slowly chipped away.

When we experienced our first loss, I spent hours and many sleepless nights scouring the internet for hope. What I got instead was a bunch of medical articles and lots of forum posts from women in different stages of miscarriage. What I didn't find and desperately wanted was answers to what now, what happened after. I am a planner, and I will research a topic until I know everything there is to know. What happened instead was I was left feeling very alone in my grief. I felt ashamed of the anger I felt, guilty for the jealousy, afraid of how desperately lost I felt at time and (excuse my language) but bat sh*t crazy... how quickly I could go from completely normal to crying uncontrollably in the middle of the grocery store aisle.

I started writing about our devastating losses, even though it felt wrong and too open and honest to share on the Internet. In retrospect, I am not sure I ever expected anyone actually to read what I had to say. Writing can be therapeutic for me, and I thought, "Maybe if I just get these things out of my head I will be able to move on."

What it gave me in return was so much more. It brought many people into my life I had never expected it would and opened up the hearts of other hurting mommas who just felt understood by hearing my crazy intense thoughts vomited in the midst of our grief. It gave me a sisterhood of women who understood, gave me a judgment-free zone to be me when I wasn't at my best and permission to feel the pain I was trying so desperately to cover up.

My first piece of advice would be to remember we all have corners we need people to be in with us. Let them. Invite them in. You'll be amazed, when you do, at how many corners we all share, and how much we can brighten them up when we're all in them together. It is amazing what will happen when you do. Everyone has something in her journey worth sharing. Something that would help someone deepen their understanding of a friend's plight, something that would change an opinion, something that would make someone feel less alone in their struggle, something that would open up a new door for someone else, something, something, something.

    I am who I am today and where I am in my grieving for so many reasons - one of the most important is: I have had people walk alongside me and share their journeys with me. Journeys that, at the time, might have seemed to be unrelatable, but eye-opening all the same. These journeys helped me think differently and decide to act differently because someone close to me or someone I barely knew was willing to share their experiences with me. Someone's willingness to trust me with their deepest thoughts and feelings that made me feel less alone in having the same ones. They didn't hog their journey all to themselves for fear of judgment, misconception, fright, or guardedness. And although I hate that I had to be a part of the one in four statistics, I am grateful that I now can empathize and have such a strong understanding of something I may otherwise not.

    I remember telling my mom after finally opening up about our experience with others that while it was a hard road, it was one with many people along the way who had experienced it too. Individuals who were always ready to lend a kind word, an ear to listen to me vent, or a helpful direction to head in, or a support hug at the drop of a hat. Mom expressed that she didn't think infertility, miscarriages, adoption and loss had been as prevalent when she had kids, or maybe, she added people just didn't talk about it.

Ah-ha. I think that's it. I think people "hogged" their journeys a little more. It's hard for me to understand why. After all, I'm a product of the "let's share everything" generation. I can't imagine trying to get pregnant and experiencing the losses that we have over the last several years, walking the adoption journey with its roller coasters with no one knowing, but instead wondering behind closed doors, "Why I am the only one?" It makes me frustrated for women thirty, forty, fifty years ago that didn't feel like they had a wide-spread support system, a sisterhood, a camaraderie with others dealing with the same issues; that it might have been considered taboo to talk openly about, something so near and dear to most women.

I consider it a privilege to have access to those resources. They are personal and honest and raw compared to the clinical, sometimes cold, and often impersonal feel of just seeking advice elsewhere. When I need real advice, really real advice, I want to talk to other women who have experienced loss, moms who have experienced the same things I've experienced and can speak to them in unfiltered and totally honest ways. And I want to do that too for other people. Here's the thing, in not keeping my journey to myself, in putting it out there, I might be advocating the end of miscarriages and infant loss being such a taboo subject, but my real goal is someone else coming to a realization they aren't alone. But I'm also getting a lot of encouragement, wisdom, things to think about, and camaraderie from those who respond to my journey too.

The more I share, the more I process, the more I learn and better understand the struggles that so many are facing from infertility and the loss of a child and adoption woes. There's this piece in my heart that is missing, and instead of trying to fill it with things of this world, I want to share it – just in case a piece of yours is sitting vacant.

The more I share, the more I realize I am not alone in this pain and loss.

They say the loss of one's child is the hardest thing you will ever experience and in my 26 years of life I would say that to be true. I wish I could tell you that the grief goes away, but my goal here is to be raw and honest with you.

I could give you the details of my many miscarriages or the stories of birth mothers who have changed their minds, and the stories of those losses, but I want to give you permission to grieve in any way you want! I don't want you to feel alone, being alone during in your grief and the question, "Is this normal?" can sometimes be worse than the grief itself. You're heartbroken and struggling with grief and for very real reasons. Do not let anyone downplay how real this is for you. No matter the size of that baby at the time of the loss, it was a life and a life that was conceived in love and genuinely wanted and desired. Your heart is hurt. You were left with empty arms, and your body is forever changed.

I find myself going through different stages of grief dealing with our loss. At times, I feel crazy with emotions. Grieving is a healthy process; brushing your true feelings under the rug is not. Walking through each step of grieving and feeling your emotions is the best thing you can do. So often in this world, we think of being "emotional" as a bad thing. In fact, it's not. I'm one of those who is learning that every day.

My point is this: give grieving its time, and the time it's due, and if it takes a while, so be it. Don't feel bad for not "getting over" something quick enough. There are no time limits! At times, I am guilty of feeling like I have grieved for too long about our losses. But really? I believe that when you give yourself that time to feel, then you can experience the joy and happiness on the other side. I know I have.

So, I want you to know that you're not alone if you feel lonely in this grief. You're not alone if you feel afraid in general or are afraid of your thoughts or emotions or for what the future holds; you are not the only one. Know there are others who are in your same shoes and know that given the opportunity they will give you all the grace you need. The amount of forgiveness that was offered by those I leaned on as they allowed me to be free in my feelings was my lifeline. Know that you are not broken or damaged goods, you are not any less of a woman or wife, and you are not any less beautiful, you are not any less important, for what has happened with your pregnancies. I have spent countless hours repeating this to myself. Some days I could use a sticky note on my forehead that says it, so when I look in the mirror or see my reflection, I see that message instead of the shame, regret, and guilt that often come with what I see back in the mirror.

While yes there are physical reminders like scars and just changes in my body that are a product of my pregnancies, but the tricks my mind plays on me are the cruelest. I would have done anything to have healthy pregnancies and healthy children. It's not my fault. I didn't do anything wrong. And I shouldn't be punished in any way, especially emotionally, for that. My body betrayed me, not the other way around. I know this; just as I'm sure in your heart, you see this is the truth too. But in those moments of sadness and grief however often or far between, they are those lies that creep in and you play the blame game with yourself and that big "WHY ME" questions it takes over.

I don't know you, but know that no matter where you are in your grieving you are doing a remarkable job at moving forward with the horrible circumstances you've been forced to endure. I'm so proud of you, and so inspired by you. I don't want you to believe you're anything less because of the pregnancy losses; you never asked for any of this to happen. You just want a healthy living child. And that's such a beautiful and wonderful thing. There's no shame in the rocky path you have had to take to get closer to motherhood. It seems to me that you're doing your best. And I hope you can see victory in that. I'm just so sorry that you have to face all of this.

I am so grateful that so many have trusted me with their stories and I hope you will trust others with yours. They have all have had an enormous impact on my life. And I'm so thankful that we're able to stand together in remembering these babies. I pray that you'll have the courage to talk and write about your experiences, too. You just never know whom you can reach out and touch.

4 JADE

Jade is historically known to be an imperial stone and traditionally, bright green in color. Green is the color of life and fertility. But what happens when the natural fertility you are used to backfires on you with no warning? Such is the story of our Jade.

I was 40 years old pregnant with my fifth child. This pregnancy was a surprise because I was using a non-hormonal, over-the-counter contraceptive. However, I could tell from the beginning something was very wrong. This experience was my first with miscarriage, and it was unexpected given my history.

I had my first child at 20 years old. I was considered high risk because I was not gaining any weight during the pregnancy. The pregnancy itself was uneventful, and I did not experience any difficulties. As a matter of fact, I went to Six Flags and rode the roller coaster despite the fact that the sign read that it prohibited pregnant women. I was so young and felt I was invincible. I remained very active throughout this pregnancy. Working long hours on my feet at the grocery store and catching buses to and from work.

Around the eighth month, I began to gain weight. I blew up overnight out of nowhere. The last month of that pregnancy I finally gained 20 pounds. It was all baby of course because he weighed seven pounds. The delivery was quick and only required a total of six hours labor, and he was out. I did it all natural because I am afraid of needles and was terrified of the epidural and the big needle that was required to receive it. I passed on that experience.

Two years later, I became pregnant again (if I were not on birth control I would easily get pregnant with no problem.) I was active with this pregnancy as well, and this helped with the delivery. I was only in labor for three hours and was medicine free. After these two pregnancies, I never questioned my ability to have children and to go full term in my pregnancy.

My two sons were around the age of nine and twelve when I decided to get a tubal ligation. I was in my early 30s, and my sons were almost teenagers. I thought there was no way I was going to have any more children at this age. However, I was wrong, and I did want and had more children.

I remarried two years after receiving my tubal ligation and decided that I would reverse the procedure. During the summer of 2007, one the best doctors in my city operated on me and completed the tubal ligation reversal. It was a success! Any woman having this procedure takes the risk of not being able to have a child again because there is less tube for the egg to travel through. I was willing to take that chance.

To my surprise and the doctor's, I was pregnant less than five months after the procedure, and the pregnancy did not end in a miscarriage or ectopic pregnancy. These terms were never a consideration for me when it came to having a baby. I heard of women who may have experienced these types of situations, I just never have been or considered that I would be one myself.

When it came to miscarriages, I had talked to many women who shared that they had one or had many. They never went into detail about the experience or what they felt afterward. In my mind, I just thought they passed an underdeveloped baby at home and proceeded on with their day. It was hard to empathize or sympathize fully. When you haven't experienced something in your life, many times, you can be far removed from that experience. You are just an onlooker who hears the story, yet you have no clue to the realness of that experience.

After the reversal of the tubal ligation, I had two daughters successfully. My oldest daughter was born through an unnecessary C-section. (I could go into why I said it was "unnecessary" but not at this moment.) However, this did lead to more scar tissue in my uterus because of the surgery. My second daughter was born as a vaginal birth after C-section (VBAC), and she was full term. I was overjoyed to have both of them considering I'd had the surgery.

I became pregnant again right before my youngest daughter was turning two years old. Again, this came as a surprise because I used an over-the-counter, non-hormonal contraceptive. I did, however, wait for the full 10 minutes after I inserted to have sex as the directions instructed. Nonetheless, I began to feel sick a few weeks later, so I took a home pregnancy test. I cannot say I was excited at first to see that it was positive. I was first in shock because I used birth control and did not realize what happened initially. Nothing felt abnormal the first few weeks of the pregnancy. Around the seventh week is when things took a turn for the worst.

During sex, I began to bleed as though I was having my period. The blood was dark red, and there was an enormous amount in the bed. This sight "scared the mess" out of me because I had never experienced this with any of my previous four pregnancies. I rushed to the hospital because I knew this was not normal; however, I could not begin to tell you what I thought was happening. The doctor took a urine sample and did an ultrasound. The doctor searched for a heartbeat which seemed like for hours, however, she was not able to find one. I began to panic because I knew at seven weeks she should be able to hear something from the baby. I asked what the problem was and her response was very evasive. She stated that at this time they were not able to hear anything and that I needed to do a follow-up exam with my doctor in a few days. Well to me that wasn't enough. I needed more answers, and I needed them right now. Who wants to wait for a few days to hear about the baby and the baby's health? Surely not me!

When I went home with unanswered questions, I felt a plethora of emotions that I had never had to experience during pregnancy. I was worried about the fate of my unborn child. This feeling was killing me inside, and I just began to cry profusely and had a hard time gathering myself. My husband tried his best, but it wasn't enough. I started to feel guilty that I wasn't overly excited about the pregnancy at the beginning. I began to think God was punishing me for not being grateful for the gift he blessed us with. I kept going over the doctor's words again and again in my head and out loud. I thought this would help to figure out the secret code of what she was trying to tell me. I felt so out of control. So, I went home, hoping and praying that everything would be okay with the pregnancy.

I felt all alone because I felt that the hospital and doctors did not give me much assistance or comfort at all. They didn't refer me to a counselor who had experience with this situation. I did not want to talk to friends and family about the situation because I was still holding out on the hope that the baby would survive.

I had a follow-up appointment around nine weeks gestation to see if there was any progress at all. Once again, my doctor's office could not offer me much comfort. They could not hear a heartbeat and told me there was not much they could do at this point. They instructed me that I should go home and "just wait it out." I'm thinking, "Wait, what out?" I didn't know what to expect or what to do to prepare. No one was giving me any helpful hints. I was becoming frustrated and impatient with the whole situation. In the meantime, I'm still growing and looking as if I were pregnant. I hoped that the baby was thriving.

I was wrong! One night after I put the kids to sleep, I went into the living room to watch television. As I sat down, I felt pressure in my stomach and pelvic area. It felt like I was in labor. This pain came from nowhere, and I could barely walk or talk. It just hit me all at once. I was doubled over and confused about what to do. Should I stay home or should I go to the hospital? I didn't want to go to the hospital because they weren't much help to me the last time. Eventually, I decided to go to the hospital anyway because I couldn't take the pain anymore.

When I had talked to women in the past about their miscarriages, I never recalled anyone of them explaining that they went through this much pain. I had no clue as to what to expect. I never asked because I just assumed a clot just passed through, and it was over. How naïve of me to think this was all there was to it. What I was feeling felt like three previous times I went into labor. Except I knew this time, I was not delivering a baby that I would take home with me. I was distraught, and all I could do was lie on the bed in the hospital and cry as the baby was delivering. The doctors would not do a full pelvic exam because they knew what was happening. They gave me some medicine to help ease the pain.

The next thing I knew, I coughed, and I felt this gush of liquid and what felt like a massive clot come out of me. I told the doctor what happened and she checked underneath the covers. She said that I just delivered the fetus. She placed the fetus in a cup and sealed the top. She would not let me see the cup at all. I didn't understand why she would not let me see my baby. I was heartbroken and just all around destroyed at that moment. I could do nothing but cry.

After I had gone home, I took a shower and just lay down on the couch. I didn't talk much, and I just could not believe what just happened. I was feeling like, "Why me? Why this pregnancy?" and "What did I do wrong?" The hospital told me some things that would happen next. For example, they would give the baby a funeral, and I was welcome to come. Ironically the funeral was on my birthday. I do not deal well with death or funerals, so there was no way that I was attending the funeral. I couldn't handle it at all. I wondered so many things like what the baby would look like, if it was a girl or boy and what would I have named him/her. I didn't talk much about this experience for a while after it happened. I began to open up about it months later.

I experienced a second miscarriage with a pregnancy after the last miscarriage. Everything appeared to be going fine. However, a few weeks into the pregnancy, the bleeding began, and I knew this time that something was wrong. I didn't even go the hospital because of my last experience. I bled for few days, so I figured that everything had passed, the miscarriage was complete, and it was over. I think I avoided the doctors and the whole situation because I didn't want to think about it again. It is not a good feeling to lose a child, and I think I was going into denial. Weeks went by, and I thought nothing of it.

Then one night I felt that pain again. I was shocked and surprised because I thought I had already had the miscarriage. Well, I was wrong. I began to bleed profusely, and the pain was unbearable, just like before. I was back and forth to the bathroom bleeding and in pain. I think as I sat on the toilet I unknowingly passed the fetus. This experience was different than the last one because I bled more and was in pain for days. I just stayed in bed and relaxed for a few days. I didn't initially go to the doctor because of the many circumstances that were going on in my life at this time. I also think I was just trying to avoid the whole situation. I didn't understand why this kept happening to me and what could I have done differently. I felt this was it, I'm over 40, and I obviously can't have any more children. I didn't want to go through this again. So, I made an appointment to go to the doctor and get on birth control.

I didn't think I could get pregnant right away after the miscarriage but to my surprise I did. I was feeling sick one morning, and before everyone was up, I decided to run to the store to get a home pregnancy test. I thought, "Surely, I am not pregnant. I just don't feel well." Besides I was about to get on birth control, right? Well, I looked at the stick, and what do you know, it was positive. I was so happy and thanked God for another opportunity to try again.

This pregnancy was monitored very closely by the doctors and myself. I had an episode where I began to bleed at the beginning, and my thoughts were, "Here we go again." The doctor checked me when I went in for a visit. However, she said this time around she heard a heartbeat. I was so happy! After that one episode of bleeding, I prayed, and it never happened again. I gave birth to a beautiful, healthy, baby girl. Even though prayed the other times I know God has a plan for everything and He knew what was best!

5 ROYAL

The color blue is elegant and regal. It is the color of serenity and truth. Blue is also the color associated with sadness and grief. Our Royal experienced exponential grief during the time she shares with us. Read to see how she endured.

The year of 2007 started off with so much promise for my little family and me. It began with so much excitement. I was 28 years old and had recently discovered that I was pregnant with our second child. We were in our 4th year of marriage (although we are no longer married) and I was in my 6th year of teaching. I had just had my first promotion with the direct sales company I'd been with for a few years. Our son, my smiling, laughing ball of squirmy energy, had just turned two in December. We had a beautiful home with two empty bedrooms, and we lived in a great neighborhood

with good schools. I even had the world's sweetest beagle. No really. I know it sounds crazy, but Paddington was a saint. One time, I heard

71

him suddenly start whining and crying from the family room. I walk into the room to discover my son was using Paddington's floppy ear as a teething ring. He had just cut two perfectly sharp bottom teeth on the same day. They looked like little pieces of rice, but those things were sharp. Paddington sat there, crying out in pain, but never once did he ever try to move away, growl, bark...He'd just let him do it. When he slept in his bouncer, Paddington sat by him, guarding him. When he would cry, Paddington would tug at our pant legs to make us get to our son faster. Somehow, he just made the whole family picture feel a little more...perfect. The only thing we were missing was the picket fence, which was against HOA rules.

It was the perfect time to start working on a little sister for our son. We had just begun trying. I hadn't expected for us to conceive so quickly. Everything was lining up so well. I had good friends and family around me since I had lived in the area my entire life. I had a fantastic babysitter lined up for when it was time for me to go back to work. A retired pediatric surgical nurse, right there in my neighborhood. She had cared for my son until it was time for him to start daycare and he adored her. Plus, it was only a 1-minute drive from my house to her home daycare. Like I said, it was a good time for us to try to expand our little family.

I hadn't cared about the sex of the baby during my first pregnancy, but this time...oh, this time I was determined that I was going to have a girl. I'd selected her name the instant I'd found out that I was pregnant. I already knew her name ... Stephanie. I wasn't even going to pick out boy names. There was no possibility that she would be anything but a girl, as far as I was concerned. A beautiful, happy, chubby baby girl. Oh, yes. I had everything planned out perfectly.

But then the plan began to change. I'd had to announce my pregnancy much sooner than I was expecting because I was showing so quickly. I'd gotten so big so fast that we thought, maybe it's twins! I had begun to show at about five weeks, and I was in maternity clothes by the time I was eight weeks pregnant. I had always heard that you get big faster after your first pregnancy, but this still seemed incredibly fast to me. I had assumed that I'd at least be close to completing my first trimester before I'd start to show. I had been more than six months pregnant with my son before I had to start wearing maternity clothes, much to my dismay. But my quick growth hadn't really caused us any sense of alarm. It actually added an extra sense of excitement. You see, my fraternal twin sister had passed away just days after our birth. The entire family was thrilled at the idea of twins having twins.

I had a few abnormalities with the pregnancy. I scheduled my appointment for an official pregnancy test at the doctor's office as soon as I had a positive home pregnancy test. Somehow, the blood test came back inconclusive, and I would have to have a second test done, which meant I'd have to push back my initial appointment because I couldn't schedule a prenatal appointment unless the blood test confirmed the pregnancy. At that moment, I thought, "Something's wrong." but I firmly pushed the thought out of my head. After all, this was the best planning and the best timing I'd ever executed. I had a boy, and I was going to have a girl. Period. My first appointment was unremarkable, which was incredibly comforting. It made it easy for me to go on being blissfully happy with my pregnancy and happily planning for the future.

On another occasion, I had been out to dinner with my parents and brothers for my mom's birthday. We were at one of our favorite seafood restaurants and I was about to get my favorite meal. I suddenly had a strong urge to use the bathroom. As I used the bathroom, my lower abdomen began to cramp more. Had I eaten something wrong earlier in the day, or was something wrong? Was I about to go into labor in the seafood restaurant bathroom? Was this labor? I stayed in there for what felt like forever. Praying and willing the pain to stop, not because of the discomfort, but because I didn't want anything to be wrong with my baby. And I couldn't think of anything worse than ruining my mother's birthday dinner, not to mention more embarrassing, than being rushed to the hospital from the bathroom of a restaurant. Slowly, I began to feel better. Then, when I wiped, I saw what vaguely looked like mucus, but just with that one wipe. I knew if I called the doctor, she'd have me come in. I told myself that if I saw it again, I'd definitely call, but for the moment, I was going to put on my happy face and go eat my diner.

It never happened again. I felt fine and kept getting bigger, a fact that gave me much comfort. After all, if my baby was growing, she had to be okay, right? I chalked the experience in the bathroom up as indigestion or something. Maybe I hadn't seen any mucus at all. At my next scheduled visit, the doctor asked if I had been spotting and had me schedule a sonogram as a precaution. My mind instantly flashed to that moment in the bathroom. I hadn't been spotting, and had been feeling fine. In fact, I was excited. I was going to get to see my baby already!

The day of the sonogram, I arrived cheerfully for my appointment with my bladder full, as requested only to find that they were running behind schedule. I sat in the waiting area casually chatting with the woman beside me. We joked about the long wait and talked about our families until I was called. The doctor and I pleasantly chatted as she began the sonogram. But as the procedure progressed, she talked and smiled less and less. I remembered from my pregnancy with my son that there should have been a flutter ... some movement ... something. But everything looked still. "I'm having a hard time finding the baby's heartbeat." she'd told me with a tight smile. "I'm going to do a vaginal sonogram. Why don't you go to the bathroom first?" It took me a moment to process, because the voice in the back of my mind told me, "She's hiding something. Something's wrong."

When the doctor sent me to the bathroom to empty my bladder, which was about ready to explode, I already knew what she was about to tell me. I could already feel what she knew, even though I tried to tell myself to be positive. "You're not a doctor," I told myself as I attempted to keep my composure. I teared up as I used the bathroom, knowing that it was about to be the worst possible thing that could happen, as far as I was concerned. I connected the dots through my 11 weeks of pregnancy. First, the blood test had been inconclusive; and there was the incident in the bathroom. Suddenly, my being so big so fast didn't seem like a good thing. As I tried not to cry, I began to think, "I'm going to have to walk out of there, call my job, tell them ... tell everyone. I'm going to have to drive like a rational person. I'm going to have to 'man up.' I'm going to have to drive around as a coffin for my dead baby." And that's exactly what happened. Just like that, 2007 took a nosedive.

Suddenly, the baby bump that had given me so much joy, the bump I loved to look at in the mirror, the baby bump I that I was planning shopping trips for, was now a visual reminder that I had lost a baby. It was a visual reminder of my sorrow. And I was still growing. I walked back into the waiting room, and upon seeing the woman I'd been chatting with just 30 minutes earlier, I crumbled. She took me in her arms and held me as I cried in the waiting room. She rocked me the way my mother did, the way my grandmother had. Without saying a word. I didn't have to tell her what had happened. It was evident to everyone in the room. When I look back, I can see every woman in that room had placed a protective hand on their prized baby bumps. I can feel the prayers, "Please God, don't let that happen to me. Please let my baby be okay."

For me, that prayer was not to be. The vaginal sonogram revealed that the baby had died at about eight weeks of pregnancy, right around the time I had the incident in the restaurant. My body had failed to abort the dead fetus. What I'd had was called a partial molar pregnancy. Two sperm had fertilized the same egg. There was nothing that could have been done to save the baby because it had the wrong number of chromosomes and never had a chance. And on top of that, my body was forming these grape-like tumors at a pretty quick rate, which was the reason I'd gotten so big so fast. I'd have to have tests run for a while, and I'd have to wait a year before I could try to get pregnant again. And I would have to have a dilation and curettage or a D&C (which is basically an abortion) since the fetus hadn't passed on its own. I had to walk around pregnant with a dead baby for an additional week and a half.

My then husband was not known for being sympathetic ... or empathetic ... or terribly involved. You may have noticed that I haven't mentioned him too much. That wasn't an error; he wasn't present during the events I've described to you. I was married to the type of man who would hear me fall down an entire flight of stairs and continue to watch television without even casting a glance to see if I was still alive. I'm not saying this to badmouth, just want to give you some insight as to my frame of mind. I wasn't expecting any emotional support from him, so I was surprised when he cried with me when we got home. He held me until I cried myself to sleep. That was about the extent of the comfort he gave me, but it was exactly what I needed, and I'm forever grateful to him for his support on that day.

Just before the sonogram, I'd learned that the grandmother of one of my closest friends had passed and her funeral was that coming weekend. To make matters worse, soon after receiving this news, I learned that my paternal grandmother had been diagnosed with throat cancer. She had been having trouble swallowing, and it turned out that a tumor was why. She was one of my favorite people in the entire world. She was beautiful, kind, smart, spunky, and one of a kind. She had owned a dance school, The Louise Forrest Johnson School of Dance, which was one of only two dance schools for African Americans in Atlantic City at the time. Not too many African American women had their own businesses in the 1950s, but "Mamma J" did. She was fierce and fabulous and has always been one of my greatest inspirations.

I was still carrying my dead baby, and I was still growing larger as I attended the funeral to support my friend. People kept asking me when I was due, and I'd just smile and say, "August" because I couldn't tell the truth without breaking into tears. I felt like a coffin. I couldn't lift my spirits and didn't feel like I'd ever be able to again. Not only was my grandmother dying, one of my best friend's grandmothers had died, too. After her entombment, I decided to see my maternal grandmother since she was buried in the same cemetery. It made me feel a little better, the idea that I could ask her to watch over my baby. Maybe she could find my sister, and they could all stay together and watch over each other. It was a comforting thought.

I went to the visitors' center and got a map to locate the grave. I never returned to the cemetery after Grammy's burial in June of 1999. However, we'd recently gotten a beautiful new marker made for her grave, and I wanted to see it. Only it wasn't there. I walked around the cemetery for an hour looking for it before I called my mother to tell her. That's when I discovered that my entire family was in Atlantic City visiting Mamma J. My parents had spoken to my husband to see if I wanted to ride up with them, but he'd forgotten to relay the message that they were traveling that weekend. My brothers and sister, all of my cousins, aunts, and uncles were there. Everyone was there except for me and apparently, Mamma J kept asking for me. To this day, it still puts a lump in my throat that I wasn't there during her last conscious moments. I wish I could have spoken to her, just one more time.

I went up to Atlantic City a few days later with my son and husband. My grandmother had lost consciousness the day before and was on the decline, although they weren't sure why. The surgeons said that the feeding tube had been inserted perfectly. The procedure had gone flawlessly, but my grandmother's organs were shutting down one by one and it was just a matter of time. My son had gotten antsy, so he and his father had left a while earlier, but I wasn't ready to leave Mamma J's side just yet. Different family members and friends filed in and out throughout the day. I sat by her, talking to her, praying with her and holding her hands. I told her that I was there and that she didn't have to stay. That we would be okay and she didn't have to suffer.

After a while, my oldest brother came in to visit. As we sat chatting, my grandmother took one final deep, rattling breath. I'll never forget the sound of that final breath. It was unmistakable, and we didn't need the nurses or doctors to tell us that she was gone. We informed the nurse that she had stopped breathing. She used a stethoscope and said she was still breathing a little, but she was going to have the doctor talk to us. We understood what that meant, too. She didn't want to be or wasn't allowed to be the one to say it officially, but Mamma J was gone.

The doctor finally came in and confirmed what we already knew. That breath had been her last. I called my father, my aunt, and my uncle to let them know that Mamma J had passed. My parents had just left New Jersey the day before, but when my aunt arrived, I dissolved. At that moment, it was all just too much. I kept thinking that I was sitting beside my dead grandmother and carrying a dead baby. And then I dissolved into a puddle on my aunt's beautiful mink coat, and then cried harder at the thought that I might have ruined it.

The next day, I traveled back to Maryland. I still had to have the procedure. I never told my doctor about my grandmother because I didn't want her to say to me that I couldn't travel after the procedure. It was a strange procedure. I went to sleep pregnant and woke up not pregnant. I was told to expect some cramping, heavy bleeding, and to pass clumps of tissue. Of all of the symptoms described, the tissue clumps were the hardest to deal with emotionally. I'd have morbid thoughts, wondering what part of the baby it was. I'd sit and think about it for hours at a time. So rather than be sad, I decided to stay busy. I went shopping to make sure everyone was ready for Mamma J's funeral, which was three days after the D&C. The funeral was well-attended, and the funeral directors did an excellent job of making Mamma J look like herself.

I went on autopilot. I dressed like myself. I spoke like myself. I smiled at the appropriate times. I did my job. I continued to go out and do parties for the direct sales company, and I went back to work. But I was wearing a mask. Inside, I was numbed. I told everyone that I was okay. I mean, my father had just lost his mother, how was I supposed to go crying to my parents? I felt like I had to be strong, had

to be okay for them. I had to be okay for my son. I had to be okay for

my students.

Everyone wanted to hug me and tell me how sorry they were

for my losses. Everyone wanted to know how I was doing and holding

up. I felt like I had to be okay. I mean, what was I supposed to say? "I

feel like an entire section of my heart is missing, thanks for asking,

Mary."

No. I couldn't go around telling people that I felt broken. I felt

like I had to be okay. I mean, I knew women who had been through

three, four, even five miscarriages. Who was I to be distraught over just

one, especially when I had a perfect, beautiful, active 2-year-old boy?

He was such a joy with his big, bright eyes, curly hair, and infectious

laugh. He was healthy and happy and amazing, and I was so blessed

beyond measure to have him. So how dare I be sad? Didn't I know

how many women couldn't even have one baby? Hadn't I watched

several of my friends suffer terrible miscarriages, some in their second and even third trimester? Who was I to feel sad, to mourn, to be down? And since it was the only way I seemed to feel, I just decided not to feel anything at all.

Eventually, I got used to the numbness. I became so accustomed to the feeling that I didn't even realize until summer break when I had the chance to have some time to myself that I was miserable. I wasn't okay, not even close to it. I had never dealt with the emotions of January. I just stopped allowing myself to think about it. But now that I had time, I realized that I wasn't fine. It hit me suddenly one day as I stood there in the kitchen, making lunch for my son. I was miserable. I think it was some sad TV show, like a Law and Order with a murdered child or something, that set me off. I stood in my kitchen and cried. Really cried. Ugly tears; the kind where you cry so hard, that you can't even make a noise. Can't even inhale at first. I cried like that for what felt like hours. In actuality, I have no idea how much time had passed, but I didn't try to stop myself. I finally allowed myself to feel what I'd been hiding from since January. It wasn't until then that I think I began to heal.

I wish I could go back in time. Well, that's not entirely accurate because I don't want to re-live everything. I wish I could send myself a message, give myself some support and advice. I'd tell me that you don't have to pretend that you're not hurt. There's no prize for being "okay" or "fine" quickly. I should have taken some time to grieve and heal. I'd tell myself to think of myself. I didn't have to be okay for anyone. I'd tell myself that it wasn't my fault.

Even though the doctor explained what had happened with my pregnancy, even though I knew that I hadn't done any of the things that I wasn't supposed to do, I still felt deep down that there had to be some reason, something I'd done wrong to lose my baby. I didn't even realize that I'd felt that way until I'd taken the time to observe my thoughts and feelings. I'd tell myself to seek help. I would talk to my mom or some friends or even a counselor. I'd tell myself that there was no shame in grief or depression.

To anyone out there who is reading this, to anyone out there who is struggling with grief, anger, or depression, please be kind to yourself. Please take the time to grieve and heal. Take the time to love yourself. I hope that sharing my story has helped someone.

Wendy Howell

6 VIOLET

In history, violet and purple have long been associated with royalty and majesty. It is also the color people most often associate with individualism and the unconventional. Our Violet's approach to healing could be considered unconventional - but it works for her. Here is her story.

It was November 9, 2009. I knew I was pregnant but had a terrible feeling. As I woke up that morning, I had intense cramps and was beginning to spot, but thought if I ignored it it would go away. That was also the day I was meeting up with coworkers to celebrate the life of my former supervisor, Sue Cobb, who had given me my career position as a pediatric physical therapist with the Prince George's County public school system. Unfortunately, she lost her battle with cancer just a few months before, and now we were all going to participate in a walk in her honor in DC. I got dressed, put on my running shoes, and I was at the house making sure I had my phone, keys, and wallet just as I do every morning. It all seemed so routine

except for my destination.

I rode the Metro downtown by myself with the pain in my belly

growing slowly. I stood up when we reached my stop, and I had to sit

back down. But I knew this day was too important to miss, so I got off

the train, found a map that showed me where I needed to go, and

walked a few blocks shuffling my feet at a snail's pace to the start line.

Everyone else was already underway. I closed my eyes now welling up

with tears from the intense pain and the brisk air and took only eight

steps past the start line before I knew I could go no further. I didn't

want to make a scene, but I knew what was happening inside. I found a

seat on a curb and took in a deep breath as the reality hit. I was

thankful for the distraction when people I knew were finishing their

race and I was able to join them for a few minutes in the reception tent.

I didn't have much to say as so many emotions from the past and

present pains were rising to the surface, so I said goodbye and made my

way back to the metro alone.

As I write this, I sit in tears remembering that awful day. I thought it was behind me, and I have moved on as a strong woman should, but I realize I put on a happy mask each day to face the people and events, but some sadness is never gone. Maybe it's due to the recent loss of my dad, or other friends who are gone too soon, but being asked to write about that day has made me again emotional. However, I am ready to prioritize what is really important in life like my family, helping my kids experience adventures, form positive memories and hopefully ensure they will grow up to be kind, caring members of society who can make good choices and stay safe. I want to say I hope no one else will ever have to experience this, but unfortunately, I know they will. I hope that they can find comfort just as I did in loved one's arms and stay strong to move forward taking each day as it comes, whether trying again or not. Don't be in a rush to move on or make any final decisions, but be open to all of life's possibilities.

Have you ever felt guilty for not feeling guilty enough? I wasn't sure if I felt any change from that day to today, but I always felt that I didn't feel bad enough. I knew I was surrounded by people who love me and a life that I loved and had worked hard to have. My home, my job, my friends, and all of my activities kept me busy and feeling thankful for what I had. But I had seen others including my mom, various friends, and other mothers I worked with in their homes, go through the loss of a baby. All had their own ways of dealing with it, but all were completely heartbroken. I've seen some go into depression having to leave their other child or children with their mothers.

I'd seen my own mother when I was 14 years old experience a tragic loss. She had just recently told us she was expecting a third baby, and I was excited to help take care of him ... I'd get to play with real life baby doll, but then I realized I only had a few more years before I left for college. Even though I already had a little brother and was used to sharing my mom, I didn't want her to take any more of her time away from me. I know I could be a selfish brat sometimes, and I'm so sorry to my mom for that.

But worst of all I remember that day that she came in from mowing the lawn and she had that look on her face tears streaming down her eyes knowing that the baby was gone. She was so upset, and I didn't know what to do. I know everyone grieves in their own way and deals with stress in a time of chaos in a less than ideal fashion. I remember my dad getting upset and I was blaming my mom for doing yard work like she had caused the problem. Not realizing how wrong it was I proceeded to echo my dad's thoughts instead of comforting my mom in her time of need. This attitude is one of my biggest regrets for not just that moment, but all of my mom's vulnerable moments. She didn't have many. My husband refers to her as superwoman because there's nothing she can't or won't do, and she always gives everything she has, especially to her children. She drove me everywhere, gave me everything, hugged me when I was sad, kissed every boo-boo, tucked me in every night, supported me through every crazy adventure and lifted me up after every fall. That baby would've been so lucky to have her as a mom too.

It's ironic that two of my friends were going through similar situations as me on my tragic day. Another friend who had two girls already, the younger being the same age as my oldest son, had told me how excited she was to be pregnant again and then how upset she was to have lost the baby just the week before. I remember being at her house the day she took the test, and she ran out saying she was pregnant with her second. Her oldest had been the flower girl in my wedding just the week before her second birthday. That friend was at my house the day I found out I was pregnant with my first son on Halloween 2007.

Was it just a coincidence that on the same fateful day of the cancer walk, my husband and I were taking our son over to that very friend's house to play? I remember the ride down there I was trying to hold in tears from the pain and anguish of not knowing if I had lost the baby. When I got to their house, I spent a lot of time in the bathroom. She came to check on me, and I remembered bursting into tears, and she just hugged me because she knew how I felt (I think.) She had just been through it too, and she was so confident everything would be okay. She reminded me that God has a plan and everything happens for a reason, whether we understand it or like it. She seemed so strong, and so I knew I could be too. But then again, we didn't have a choice. We had other little ones relying on us, not to mention the husbands.

They just don't get it! When my husband and I first started our relationship, he said that he wanted about five children. I always knew I wanted children, but his suggestion seemed so extreme that I said, "Wait for a second, let's just take it one at a time and see how the first one goes." I think that men like the idea of making the baby and look forward to playing ball with it when the baby gets older, but don't realize the late-night feedings, the constant crying, the immense exhaustion, or the emotional distress at worrying every day about someone who relies on you for everything. They don't get the immediate bond of growing a life inside you and having that with you every day as you carry that baby in your belly. The stress over how every move you make and every food and drink you swallow can affect how this baby ends up. You try to do the best you can every day from the moment you find out, but it never seems like enough.

Please know that I think the world of my husband and love him with all of my heart. When I was ready to deliver my first son, my husband was there from the moment I felt my first contraction - using a rolling pin on my back and calming me with deep breaths (and ice cream lol). He drove us to the hospital, called our parents, heard that the experienced doctor we both loved would be on-call soon to deliver our baby, putting our minds at ease. He was with me when we got the news that our baby's heart rate was in distress and we would need a C-section, and heard Tyler's first cries. At that point we were parents, and I told him not to leave the baby's side because he was the most important now. Instantly my heart filled with joy knowing this stage was complete, but completely overwhelmed feeling I knew nothing, but our baby needed us forever! My husband cut the cord, stood by our baby as he was cleaned and wrapped, took pictures of the first time I saw him, held him, and fed him ... I was a mom! He changed diapers when I couldn't get out of bed and even long after I could. This man made me a mom, and he was the best partner I could ever hope for.

Fast forward a little over a year, and suddenly in my crisis moment, he didn't understand me and I didn't know what to say. That was hard, but we both seemed to move on relatively easy. Him with his busy job and me with hugs from my toddler and somber conversations with my parents who understood and had been there before. It was comforting to hear how my superwoman mom got through it and even better to see how it brought out such compassion from my dad. It turns out he was just so upset back in the day during his experience he just had difficulty expressing it.

It sounds so callous, but we had to move on. For me, not discussing the emotions helped me put it in the past - almost like it never happened. I feel terrible now that some days I forget it did happen, my husband and I both do, but now we have a second son and a very busy life. I don't know how we would have moved on if either of us got lost in our emotions and dwelled on that event, but being asked to talk about it helps us reflect on what seems like a lifetime ago. Life would have been different, but we wouldn't have this alternate reality to compare it to. I have to believe we would still be loving, supportive parents doing all we could for each other and our babies.

7 IVORY

White is the reflection of all colors of the visible light spectrum. To many, white is considered the color of spirituality, positivity and new beginnings. After two miscarriages and a traumatic birth experience giving birth to a special needs child, Ivory was hoping for a new beginning with her second son. But this pregnancy took her into a place of utter darkness, one that only her faith and loving family could be her rescue.

In June of 1995, I became pregnant with my second son. I didn't know at the time he was a son of course; however, my pregnancy did not come without its set of concerns. At that point, I was already the mother of one son who was born with some developmental disabilities. Finding out that I was pregnant wasn't the most exciting thing at the time, but I was grateful to have the opportunity to give Tre' a sibling. Additionally, because of my pregnancy history, combined with Tre's challenges, and my age and health, there was a lot of concern about the development of this particular baby. After my husband and I prayed and got our mindsets ready we were prepared to embrace this new pregnancy.

At about eight weeks I had to go on the search for an obstetrician. The one who delivered Tre' have retired from delivering babies, so I needed to find another person that I felt comfortable with. I was hoping to have this baby at a particular hospital. I finally found a doctor whom I liked, and she also practiced out of the hospital where I wanted to deliver the baby. She was young, beautiful, intelligent and seemed to be very attuned to what was going on.

During my first visit after looking at my history and looking at my pregnancy history, of course, she recommended that I see a perinatologist who specializes in high-risk pregnancies. It was vitally important that I see a specialist who could look very carefully at the baby so I set up the appointment. They did some initial blood work and scans and I was so early that they really couldn't tell what, if anything, was going on with the baby. They had me come back once a month every month just to check on how the baby was developing and growing.

In the interim my son Tre with progressing rapidly! He was learning how to eat orally, and we were so excited. He went from having his Early Childhood Services at home to going to into the classroom to have his Early Childhood Services. We were excited that he had a great teacher, therapists, and support system. My husband at the time was in school getting his degree in paramedic medicine, so his schedule is a little crazy. As a firefighter, he already worked 24-hour shifts. He got 72 hours of off time in between. On one of those days he had to take classes, and then the other days he had to do internship hours in a medical setting - we were two ships passing in the night. Looking back on it at that time was hectic, but he made the time to come with me to my doctor's appointments, so everything was pretty much going as it should be.

Around the fourth month of my pregnancy when I went to the perinatologist's office to get a sonogram I noticed there was a bit of concern from the doctor. The baby's heart seemed to be shifted to one side (I found out later that the heart organ is supposed to be located in the center of the chest) The doctors told me, "With the baby being so small, we can't tell you what or why that is. The only thing we can do now is continue to watch the baby, and as he or she gets bigger, we will be able to give a more definitive idea of what's going on."

Around the time I was five months pregnant, I went back in for the sonogram, and the doctor was able to confirm that the baby's heart was indeed shifted over to some degree. Additionally, the baby had a cyst on the back of his brain and with the combination of those two traits they told us that our baby had a diagnosis of a genetic disorder called "Fryns Syndrome." It was earth-shattering! I was referred to Children's National Medical Center for a fetal MRI so they could get a better look at the baby.

We were already very familiar with Children's National Medical Center because our son Tre' got most of his medical attention there. In getting the fetal MRI, I had to work in close collaboration with the genetics department at Children's. Naturally, since my son already had a geneticist at Children's, I asked to be assigned to the same geneticist. I went into my very first MRI as I felt my baby do cartwheels. After it was over the geneticist and genetic counselor told my husband and I the devastating news: not only did our baby have Fryns syndrome but his prognosis was grave. The mortality rate of neonates with Fryns was 83%, and of the ones who do live, only 15% survive their first month. Not one child has survived past the age of 6. They proceeded with the explanation by giving us two options:

Option 1: Terminate the pregnancy. At that point, I was six months pregnant. The baby was kicking, spinning, jumping, flipping and doing everything else he could while he was in there. I'd already heard his heartbeat, seen his hands, face and his head. This action was something that we just could not do; something that our belief system would not allow us to move forward with. No, we're not terminating the pregnancy.

Option 2: Continue with the pregnancy. This option was a given to us, but then there were varying possibilities with this route: I would have to carry the baby to 37 weeks. If in fact, the baby did not survive to get to 37 weeks there was a slim chance that he would even be able to survive because he was so small. If I did carry him to 37 weeks, I had to decide if I wanted to have a vaginal or cesarean birth. If I had a vaginal birth that would be easier on me (looking back, on it, I believe they counseled me to have a vaginal birth because they were pretty confident that he wouldn't survive). If I had a cesarean birth, then it would have been harder on me, but it would be easier on him. As his mother, I determined that I was going to do what works best for him (it's my job to protect him, right?).

Finally, whether I had the cesarean or vaginal birth and the baby survived after the 37 weeks, his lung was so underdeveloped they would have to do intensive interventions to inflate his lungs at birth and hope that he will be able to breathe on his own or with the assistance of a ventilator. Even with that, the cyst on the back of his brain gave us a big question mark as to how it would affect the different systems and functions within his body. That was a whole different set of questions to be answered when and only when we got his breathing under control.

As you might be able to imagine, that was a massive burden to bear. Again, I was six months pregnant with one child already who needed a lot of support. When we got in the car, we cried, prayed, and asked God what to do. We decided that we didn't want to tell a lot of people and to keep the circle of knowledge very small and tight. We didn't want our loved ones to be worried or concerned about us, and we felt like it was something that we could handle. We told our parents and our pastors, and that was it.

What bothered me the most was that we had not come up with a name for the baby. We knew that he had all these difficulties, but we believed, according to our faith, that he was healed. One of the names for God in the Bible is Jehovah Rapha which means "The God Who heals." We believe that we have divine healing in our bodies (Isaiah 53:5), and because the Bible says that the fruit of my womb is blessed (Deuteronomy 28:4), it was a done deal. We had already seen the power of God's healing virtue in our almost three-year-old. Tre was already defying the odds and performing way above expectations in spite of what the doctors had said about him - why should we believe anything less for this baby? Greg and I were driving in the car, and we started discussing it. I think he came up with the idea of giving the baby a name based on "Jehovah Rapha." I loved it! We knew we couldn't name him Jehovah because that's just blasphemous, but maybe we could just use the J and instead of calling him Rapha we can call him Raphael. So, we decided to name our second born son J. Raphael Sothern.

After that, Tre got sick and right around his birthday (December 19th). We took him out for his birthday, but he was just lethargic and had a little cold. Tre's cold got worse, and we ended up taking him to the ER at Children's to get checked out. He was sicker than we thought he was. He was admitted and treated for Respiratory Syncytial Virus (RSV). Considering his respiratory system was already compromised, this virus was more aggressive towards it and attacked his lungs. And there I was, seven months pregnant, at his bedside;

trying to work, trying to manage. You can't spend the night next to the baby, so I had to sleep in the waiting room when I stayed at night. It was rough, but we endured, and four weeks later he was discharged.

At the beginning of February, my maternal grandmother passed away after a long battle with Alzheimer's. My mom, who is an only child (and I'm my mother's only child), had to deal with burying her mother and I had to support her any way that I could. So, right after getting my baby out of the hospital and settled, we had to deal with this new challenge, but we did. After the services and burial, we were hoping things would settle down, and we looked forward to reaching week 37.

A week before I went into labor I was at church and our head intercessor and my long-time friend pulled me to the side. As the lead intercessor at church, it was her job to lead the congregation into prayer in various areas and "intercede" on behalf of others. She and her husband were also our marriage counselors during our engagement. She was so sensitive that she was able to tell something was going on with me. "I don't know what's going on with you lately," she started, "But (another intercessor) and I have been just weeping and travailing for you in prayer." Remember, we had not shared our concern with anyone, and even though she was a leader at our church, our Pastors would not have revealed that to her. I immediately broke down in tears and told her everything. She held me and prayed with me, and I could feel the weight lifting from me.

The morning of February 26, 2006, I woke up with a start, having to use the bathroom and thinking that I had wet myself while I was asleep. I ran to the bathroom and didn't realize that it was my water breaking! I began to do some quick calculation mentally, thinking "Oh my gosh my baby's not due until March 9th and it I s February 26th! It's not time yet! What week is it?" When I looked at the calendar, and I realized I was 37 weeks to the day. We made hurdle number one! I had prayed and prayed that I could make it to week 37. J Raphael waited until week 37 and decided he wanted to make his appearance!

I woke up my husband; we called our parents first so we could make arrangements for Tre', then we called 911. We had decided that Greg would drive our car and I would ride in the ambulance. I think (but can't remember) that he dropped my son Tre off at my mom's house on his way to the hospital. The ambulance came almost immediately and rushed me to the hospital of our choice, which was right next to Children's Hospital (We had to switch doctors so we would be closer to Children's. My new OB was a kind, older male who specialized in complicated deliveries.) Once your water breaks, you have to deliver your baby within 24 hours. I was already scheduled for a C-section, so everything was in place.

The ride over was quite adventurous - lights flashing, sirens blaring, and my nerves were on 100 thinking about what was to come. The medic was trying to give me an IV, but my veins were not cooperating that morning, and I was starting to get annoyed with him. When we FINALLY got to the hospital, we found out that my obstetrician was not on duty for the evening but his partner, a younger doctor, was on duty. It added to my nervousness, but what could I do?

Once we arrived the medics wheeled me in, and I was taken to labor and delivery. So many thoughts were running through my mind, but I just had to focus on God's promise - that my baby was healed, and that his name added an extra level of protection when it came to healing. I did not know what the end would be, but I had to rest in the knowledge that it would be in our favor.

While in labor and delivery the nurses prepped me, helping me change, strapping me to the baby monitor, and gave me the coziest, warmest socks. They also gave me compression socks under them - I didn't know why at the time but I figured out later - I'll let you know!

In the operating room I got my epidural, nasal cannula, and the doctors began talking Greg and me through the process. Up goes the blue sheet to block me from seeing what's going on but Greg can see everything. Then starts the pulling and tugging. As the doctor is working on me, he cut the sac and the fluid just came gushing! Everyone commented that it was an extraordinary amount of fluid in the in the amniotic sac; so much so that the centrifugal force spun my baby around! But finally, the doctor delivered my tiny, 4.9-ounce baby

boy around 6:00 a.m. The nurses began to clean him up, but because

they knew he was going to have respiratory issues from the beginning,

they were ready. They wrapped him up and showed him to me. He

was beautiful, with that thick head of curly hair - just like his brother.

He already had his nasal cannula on when they presented him to me,

but I didn't get to hold him. I gave him a soft, sweet kiss on his tiny

warm cheek and he was off to the neonatal intensive care unit (NICU)

at Children's National Medical Center (CNMC).

Many of my memories of that day are very foggy. I don't know

if it was the narcotics they gave me (I think they were gracious in their

dosage knowing what was down the road for me) or if it was the

trauma of it all. I sometimes regret that I did not journal my

experiences, but there was so much pain associated with that life event

at the time when he was born. I think I would have so much more

detail to talk about at this point, but I did not do that. Maybe it was a

good thing, because the process of writing about it has been one of the

most difficult experiences. Bringing that pain back to the forefront of my memory was difficult enough, I can't imagine what the experience would be if I had maintained all of the details.

As J. Raphael started his journey over to CNMC my husband stayed with me for a while but then followed the baby, so he would be there (in my absence) to get and give updates on J's progress and make all medical decisions. After I was finally relocated to my room, I began the daunting task of informing my family members that J. Raphael had been born. Now, remember, only a few members knew what was going on with him. Once again, the baby that I had just delivered was not at the hospital with me. Once again, I was going to be inundated with questions. After my parents, the next person I called was my brother. He was clueless as to the details but got in the car to see me. On his way to the hospital, he got into a car accident! (nothing serious!) While I'm waiting for him, my Aunt Sharon called me (my brother had called her) and started asking me questions about the baby that I attempted to answer as much as I could but really, I didn't want to respond to any at all. Once she realized I was in my room alone, she got in the car and drove to the hospital to be with me.

Eventually, the word got out and around to different people that I had the baby, he had some problems and was at CNMC. Family members began to arrive. In the meantime, I'm drifting in and out of consciousness AND fielding phone calls from Greg and other loved ones.

Around noon I got a call from Greg stating that the doctors had done all they could do to get J. Raphael's breathing stabilized, but his little lungs just couldn't take it anymore. After hours of trying, they finally looked at my husband and said, "We're not going to be able to do this any longer, you need to let us know what you want us to do." My sweet husband called me in tears. I'll never forget the sound of his voice when he called me to explain what had been happening with J. Raphael. He told me there was no possible way that the doctors could continue to manually give him oxygen (he couldn't take the ventilator) and we needed to make a decision about what we wanted to do. I said something to the effect of, "I guess the decision has already been made for us." But it was paramount for me to see my baby before he transitioned.

Well, that was a battle that sent me into even more distress. When I talked to my nurses and doctor about going over to see the baby, they looked at me like I was crazy. It was February 26th, and at 18 degrees it was the coldest day of the year. I had just had major surgery. The answer I got was not the answer I wanted. That's when I lost it.

I thought that I would not have the opportunity to see my child one last time before he passed. During my meltdown, everyone started hustling and bustling, but eventually, arrangements were made for J. Raphael to be brought back to the hospital with me. I would have an opportunity to see my baby again and hold him. I don't know who made what decision, how it was done, or who approved it and I have not had the opportunity to express my gratitude towards them for what they did, but I'm grateful that they made that decision to bring him back. There were a lot of risks involved on their part if the baby has passed away during transport and a litigious family could decide to seek legal action later on. Of course, we were not that couple. We just wanted our family to be together.

Once the confirmation came that J. Raphael was in transport, I was wheeled into the nursery of the hospital. They led me to a rocking chair, and we waited. I was so groggy and woozy, but I distinctly remember the door opening and the transport team and Greg walking in the door with my baby, pumping away with the oxygen. As they walked towards me, a nurse put a handmade knit blanket in my lap. Pump … pump ... pump. FINALLY, my sweet boy was placed in my arms. He was warm and squirmy, but he was so peaceful. In my opioid-induced haze, I sat in that rocking chair and rocked my baby.

It was the best 2 to 3 minutes of my life.

In what seemed like moments, I felt his whole-body shudder, I heard him gasp, and he was gone. And I wept softly for my sweet boy who only lived for eight hours on this earth.

In the hours and days and weeks to come my life had to go back to normal. My hospital room was busy the first day but eventually got quiet, save the cries of the newborns in the rooms around me. I was finally discharged and had to push through my grief to continue to be the mother that my living child needed. We planned a memorial service for J. Raphael, and about ten people made decisions to live their lives for Christ at the ceremony. We were so proud of the people whose lives were affected from his short time here.

As time progressed, we had the opportunity to be counseled by our ministers and reconcile our faith with our reality. Some might think that we did not get what we wanted because our baby died. Our confession was that he would LIVE and that he would be HEALED. Well, guess what? He now lives forever with the Father, and he is experiencing divine health in Heaven! Did our prayer get answered? Yes, but not in the way most would expect.

So many miracles came from this dark time in our lives. Yes, it was dark, I won't shy away from that reality. In the 25 years of us being together, I can say that it was the hardest thing we ever had to endure. We were broken but guess what - we are WHOLE! We had to bend, but we did not break. The prayers that were prayed for us shielded us from the brunt of the emotional toll we could have/should have felt during that period. Also, I gained new insight on childbirth and just how customized the womb can become for the baby it carries. That extra fluid I had? It's called polyhydramnios. My body automatically made the extra amniotic fluid because it sensed that the baby inside had issues with his central nervous system so that he would have more to protect him. Isn't that awesome?

That spring, my husband went on to graduate from college, and our Tre' had major spinal surgery - two major hurdles we had to overcome. Indeed, the strength we had tapped into during our stretch with J. Raphael showed us we could get through it. I guess that was the best thing we learned from that experience. The very thing that could have utterly destroyed us did not break us, and we came out of it stronger than before. We now view life's challenges with a different lens, one we would not have had if we did not have our J. Raphael.

The best part is if we could get through it, anyone can. I never want women to feel alone in their struggle to overcome the loss of a baby, no matter what the circumstance. You were not born to break, but to bloom. I hope that the various stories in this book have shown you that not only are you not alone in your grief, but you are a member of an enormous sisterhood of women who have encountered a rainy season. But the sun will shine again for you, just like it did for us. Find your victory through the rainbow and hold onto it for dear life.

You deserve it.

RESOURCES FOR WOMEN

• **First Candle:** First Candle, along with others who have traveled this road before you, can help you through this difficult time. 1-800-221-7437 (Counselors are available 24/7) **www.cjfirstcandle.org**	**Share Pregnancy and Infant Loss Support**: The mission of Share Pregnancy and Infant Loss Support, Inc. is to serve those whose lives are touched by the tragic death of a baby through pregnancy loss, stillbirth, or in the first few months of life. **www.nationalshare.org**
• **Count the Kicks**: Available as an app, Count the Kicks is a safe and simple way to help monitor baby's well-being. It teaches expectant mothers how to monitor and track their baby's movements daily in the third trimester of pregnancy with the goal of reducing stillbirth. **www.countthekicks.org**	**Center for Loss in Multiple Birth (CLIMB):** For parents who have experienced the death of one or more, both or all of our twins or higher multiples at any time from conception through birth, infancy and childhood. **www.climb-support.org**
• **Common Care Loss Support:** Common Care Loss Support is a support group for those who have suffered miscarriage, stillbirth or early infant death and for those who experience pregnancy after loss. **www.common-care.com**	• **Grieve Out Loud: Pregnancy and Infant Loss Q&As.** Offering some comfort in real life answers to some of your real-life questions. **www.grieveoutloud.com**
• **Born Still:** Support for grieving parents **www.angelfire.com**	• **Healthy Birth Day**: Dedicated to the prevention of stillbirth and infant death through education, advocacy, and support. **www.healthybirthday.org**

ABOUT THE AUTHOR

LaTanya S. Sothern has been an educator for over 20 years. She is a passionate supporter of families of children diagnosed with disabilities, and it is her mission to help them get services appropriate for their needs. A native Washingtonian, she holds a Bachelor of Arts in Public Communication and Economics from The American University and a Master of Arts in Teaching with a concentration in Early Childhood Education from Howard University. She is certified in Early Childhood Education, Special Education, and School Administration; achieved National Board Certification (Early Childhood Generalist); and is the C.E.O. and Owner of Sothern Education Solutions, LLC – offering special education consulting, workshop presentation, and public speaking. Ms. Sothern currently serves as an administrator in the Prince George's County Public School system.

Her first book, *The Birth of an Advocate: How My Son Helped Me Find My Voice*, chronicles the story of her oldest son's first year of life as she and her husband learned to manage his various special needs. It was as featured at both the NAACP and The Congressional Black Caucus conventions in 2017.

She is happily married to her husband Greg and they reside in Prince George's County, Maryland with their two sons, Thomas III (Tré) and Quinton.

CONTRIBUTORS

Michelle L. Cole

 Michelle L. Cole was born and raised in Washington, DC and married her childhood sweetheart in 1985. But after losing five pregnancies, they divorced in 1995. Michelle then began her career working as a Government Contractor managing Government and Military travel in 2006. This career has taken her to Ft. Eustis in Newport News, VA, Army Corp of Engineer in New Orleans, LA and Atlanta, GA. She now works as a Travel Manager for a Government Contracting company at Ft. Bragg Army Base in North Carolina. Since she struggled for years with infertility issues, Michelle's passion has been to educate and support other women dealing with such issues. Her desire is for all women to live out their dreams of parenthood by any means God provides.

Vianca Smith

 Vianca Smith is the mother of Zoe Smith (4) and Jamal D. Smith (2) and has been married to her high-school sweetheart, Jamal, for 10 years. A native of Washington, DC, Vianca has served children for 14 years as an early childhood educator. Passionate about children, education, and ministry, she has also served her church, Spirit of Faith Christian Center, as a teacher and director of curriculum. Her faith, grounded in the word of God, gave her strength to endure losing one child while believing for the survival of the other who remained in her womb. This gave her courage to tell her story and encourage women suffering in silence over the loss of an unborn child.

Kelsey Freeman

I am 27 years old and married to the guy who stole my heart from the moment that he opened the car door for me at 2 am. I would be a full-time student and volunteer if it was socially acceptable! So, instead I own a Public Relations and Social Media Marketing firm and serve as the youth director at our church. This let's me sharing my heart, faith, and love of words with others. I'm a night owl, politics and sports junkie, some of favorite adventures have happened with characters in a book and if you want to make my day, bring me coffee and enchiladas.

Aisha Wilson

Aisha Wilson is a mother of five beautiful children: Khari 24, Diallo 21, Asiyah 8, Anisah 6, Azizah 2. She is a single mother who has lived in Maryland for the past three years. She was born in Chicago and moved to St. Louis when she was five years old. She has been in education for over 15 years. She is passionate about early childhood education and is a kindergarten teacher in the Prince George's County Public School system. After losing two children after the age of 40, Ms. Wilson has grown in her awareness about miscarriages and is eager to help others cope with it.

Aviyah A. Forrest

Aviyah A. Forrest is a lifelong resident of the state of Maryland. She lived in Prince George's County for more than 30 years. She currently lives in Baltimore with her two beautiful children. She has been a public-school teacher for nearly 20 years and is a National Board-Certified Teacher. She is an avid horseback rider, and in her younger years she even competed on her college team. Summer is her favorite time as it brings a much-needed break from the school year and lots of time with friends eating Maryland blue crabs. Aviyah began writing after a very difficult period in her life and has never stopped. She currently has a novel, *...So She Walked Away,* available at www.AviyahAForrest.com.

Wendy Harrell

I am Wendy Harrell, a 40-year-old proud wife and mother of two amazing boys. When I'm not team mom, assistant coach, den leader, or secretary/assistant to my talented and hard-working husband, I work as a pediatric physical therapist in the Prince George's County school system and at the Prince George's Community College Children's Developmental Clinic. Working with many children with special needs and their families has taught me to be patient, compassionate, and try to always find strength during times of struggle. I give credit to my parents: I believe I am who I am today based on the values they instilled in me and the encouragement they gave me. I strive to be as driven, selfless, and caring as them in order to make this world a happier place for everyone!

For more information on this or other books, education services, or speaking engagements, visit:

www.sothernsolutions.com
240-245-7647

Instagram: @sothernsolutions
Twitter: @sothernsolution
Facebook: **Sothern Education Solutions, LLC**